Milan Architecture
The city and Expo

To the dear "insufferables" Carlo and Ermelinda

Maria Vittoria Capitanucci

Milan

Architecture
The city and Expo

Skira

Cover
Arata Isozaki with Andrea Maffei Architects
Allianz Tower
(photo Alberto Fanelli)

Editor
Luca Molinari

Design
Marcello Francone

Editorial coordination
Vincenza Russo

Editing
Anna Albano

Layout
Paola Ranzini

Translation
Elizabeth Burke
and Kathleen Hannan,
NTL, Florence

First published in Italy
in 2015 by
Skira Editore S.p.A.
Palazzo Casati Stampa
via Torino 61
20123 Milano
Italy

www.skira.net

Printed and bound in Italy.
First edition

ISBN: 978-88-572-2854-9

Distributed in USA, Canada, Central & South America by Rizzoli International Publications, Inc., 300 Park Avenue South, New York, NY 10010, USA.
Distributed elsewhere in the world by Thames and Hudson Ltd., 181A High Holborn, London WC1V 7QX, United Kingdom.

Contents

General coordination
Alessia Mendichi

Presentations and critical evaluations
Alfio Distefano *A.D.*
Camilla Galloni *C.G.*
Roberta Marcaccio *R.M.*
Maria Giulia Mazzari *M.G.M.*
Alessia Mendichi *A.M.*
Valentina Mometto *V.M.*
Giulia Piatti *G.P.*
Domenico Sorrentino *D.S.*
Marco Trussardi *M.T.*

Many thanks to those who contributed to this volume
Simone Cola
Susanna Legrenzi
Ilaria Valente

Many thanks also to
Luisa Collina
Stefano Guidarini
Marco Imperadori
Fulvio M. Zendrini

Outskirts of Milan

Greater Milan

Ilaria Valente *

Milan on the threshold of Expo: city design and architecture

Milan is a city that is changing quickly. Now, at the beginning of 2015, it is probably possible to critically measure the consignment and completion, sometimes partial, of major urban projects conceived in the late seventies and nineties and the latest achievements of CityLife and Porta Nuova, which date to the beginning of this decade and are now being completed. Parts of the city were born out of the redesigning of the vast disused industrial and infrastructural areas whose creation corresponds to the spreading and crisis of the urban design. Parallel to this, the city's fabric has changed due to later hybrid additions. The resulting picture is a complex one and assimilation and integration are still in question as well as the opinion on the consistency and quality of individual architectural projects. However, a season has ended, a season in which construction appeared to be mainly tied to an unambiguous convergence of economic interests and a hypertrophic conception of urban growth.

Against this backdrop, Expo 2015, with the construction of the fence in Rho-Pero, the specific building projects and infrastructures, is an ideal threshold. It urgently raises the question of the future of its areas and the transformative potential that its legacy could bring with a different model of development that the city will have to adopt over the next few years.

The position of the Expo site itself in relation to Milan and its territory may indicate unprecedented issues and potentials: first and foremost the scales involved in redesigning the city, its varied and open spaces, agricultural soils, the residual spaces now involved and incorporated in the shape of the city, as well as the various degrees of compactness and dispersion of the fabric that make it up.

The terms of the discussion could revolve around an issue, probably now central to architectural and urban design: that of recognition and the proper relationship required each time it is necessary to use existing and potential resources to create different and important resources.

In addition to the due attention to containing the consumption of natural resources, energy, soil, it is necessary to recognize the composite heritage of the architectural, urban, and environmental resource, or the consignment of artificialization works that make up the living space transformed over time. The notion of resource can then be expanded and declined, because the architectural and urban design should act, prospectively, on two fronts: the consistency of the technical choices for the relationship to energy and environmental resources and recognition and enhancement of the forms of space, therefore the resources deposited in the territory.

Therefore, a possible strategy that could be applied to contemporary contexts is under discussion. These contexts often seem indecipherable be-

following pages
Grazia Toderi, *Milan*, 2003
video projection, loop,
DVD variable sizes, colour,
sound
edition of 4
courtesy of Galleria
Giò Marconi, Milan

cause they are ridden with processes of obsolescence that erase their character or, conversely, full of urban traces, buildings, figures and materials. The risk related to the progressive abandonment of sometimes vast parts of the city and its buildings is their systematic demolition, a flattening of differences through repeated operations that obliterate the weak traces, operations that reveal the vulnerability of the historical condition as a result of globalization.

In architectural and urban design practise it is therefore necessary to reaffirm the ethical and civil content aimed at remedying the aporias and the dissipation induced by the homologative logic of globalization, working towards a critical reconstruction, as a commitment and civil duty of architecture.

In the dialectic between the consolidated parts, where traces and meanings are condensed, and the short-lived parts of the city, in which the generative role is played by waste, debris, and ruins, it seems possible to reconstruct connecting tissue by looking again for the hidden connections and activating "weak" relationship networks. This can be the basis of a different design logic in the transformation process: specific projects which test various degrees of transformation in fabrics and buildings, through projects of replacement, but also maintenance, reuse, and recycling. At the same time, work on public spaces and relationship can be a new perspective for urban design, no longer understood as imposing, but as a reconstruction of a new rationality that shifts from recognition of the traces, the sediments, of the implicit structures by reusing them again and giving them an active role in the contemporary world, redeeming and regenerating them.

Therefore, understanding the architectural project as a careful reading and writing of places now appears necessary: the project can only evaluate the oscillation of the duration of fabrics and buildings, assuming their instability, accepting the potential reversibility, proceeding with care in resolving even the emergency conditions that, with their different nature and different purposes, increasingly characterize changes in today's landscapes and settlements. In this way, the architectural project can consciously direct the urban rebuilding processes, the rebuilding of settlements, and environmental projects for a better quality of urban life.

The critical repertoire of projects in the volume could be a useful piece to the puzzle for Milan, helping us to think carefully about the city's architecture once again.

*Dean of the School of Architecture at the Politecnico di Milano

*Simone Cola**

Project quality among regulations and practice

The abundance of transformations taking place in contemporary Milan in terms of number and in certain cases, also in terms of quality, highlight a rather particular economic, political, cultural and social context that very probably has no parallel in the rest of the country.

Analysing the methods that were recently used to carry out a series of major interventions in Milan, it is worth taking some time to reflect on the complex and contradictory relationship that exists in Italy between regulations and project quality, and on how, in general terms, the actions of public and private clients are conditioned by a frame of reference of this type.

This occurs because in recent decades, Italy, the European nation with the largest number of architects and renowned designers, has demonstrated a rather modest attitude towards promoting project design culture, since, unlike other neighbouring countries, it has not been able to sufficiently promote the great heritage of experience and expertise ingrained in its history and culture.

The problem regarding the overall lack of a shared national project is obviously quite complicated and not a subject for discussion in this context, without succumbing to excessive simplification. However, it is obvious that in the last few decades, the lack of a clear-cut line of reference has determined an ongoing incapacity to have any systematic impact on the protection and promotion of the territory, environment and architecture.

Seen in this light, government, national, and local laws and provisions have rarely focussed on an idea of widespread architectural quality, generally acknowledging European directives in the field of competition, market and profession without according close attention; this has led to facilitating and encouraging indiscriminate recourse to maximum reductions in project design and work execution costs without identifying the instruments able to guarantee, at different levels, the quality of the work itself.

Comparing the two Italian cities that, at the beginning of the millennium, were considered to have reflected on the question more deeply, it is impossible not to notice that while the vast urban transformation process in Turin, from urban planning to a conspicuous system of interventions, was strongly controlled by public administration, the Milanese project differs for the role played by an attentive private clientele, in certain cases substantial, not only for the profitability (revenue generating) content of the works.

In fact, wending their way through the labyrinth of residential, tertiary, university or religious building practices, in Milan, private individuals and promoters have given life to a series of initiatives that are extremely significant, not only in the quality of different architectural projects, but in their capacity to make a positive contribution to the transformation of the urban fabric.

In this respect, it is important to underline how some of these interventions are the result of mainly invitational competition procedure that have placed in comparison different possible projects; on the contrary, interventions managed directly by local administration and institutions are far fewer and very rarely subject to invitational competition processes.

On observing what has been the largest work site undertaken in Europe and which has formed one of the driving forces of the Milanese urban renewal process, it should be noted how, even with these transformations and Expo 2015 projects, the public body customers have shown little desire to set up project design contests, finding it a struggle to accredit the quality of the interventions in question.

With the exception of the Italian Pavilion, for which a rather botched-up call for bids was announced, and the Expo Gate communications structure, almost no projects were assigned through those invitational competitions that the architectural community was expecting and that would have been an absolutely legitimate assumption for such an important event.

Without going into detail about all the complex organisational and judicial episodes connected with Expo 2015, it should be noted however how the Italian bureaucratic, administrative, and organisational system connected with public works has for the umpteenth time missed the opportunity to transform a huge event financed by the public into a flywheel for promoting the disciplinary culture and capacity of Italian architects.

In this sense, from the viewpoint of the quality of the assigned public projects, the result of the Expo 2015 venture shows that, while various participants called for invitation contest bids to assign the project design of the national pavilions, all the Italian public works were organised through complex and often inefficient procedures of the Italian public contract system.

As we are well aware, although fortunately with some exceptions, in recent years this system has generally resulted in rather mediocre public project design and construction quality, producing a sadly notorious series of scandals that include, among others, the contracts connected with the Venice Mose project, the world aquatic championships in Rome, and reconstruction after the Aquila earthquake.

Italian regulations concerning contracts for project design and construction of building works are characterised by an extremely complex and constantly modified contract code system (the *Codice dei Contratti*, composed of 273 articles and 43 attachments was modified by 44 different standards and 15 converted laws; taking into account only the variations converted to law, there have been 545 including modifications, integrations, and substitutions, with only 114 articles remaining unaltered). The regulations are structurally unable to accredit the quality and trigger true competition among various projects where unfortunately, preference is given to competition among designers' sales volume or the number of employees in the architectural studios.

In this truly discouraging context, where a distorted self-referential legislation, alien to true project design quality, accumulates chaotic procedures and is often the harbinger of appeals and controversy; a context where precedence is given to personal curricula rather than to new ideas and expertise, in comparison to the national reference frame, we must applaud the great significance and exceptional role of the ConcorriMi platform promoted by the PPC Order of Architects of the Province of Milan, with the Municipality of Milan and the collaboration of the Order of Engineers.

An efficient management information system for the various stages of a "call for bids" model made it possible to organise three international project design contests in only a few months, with reduced time frames and exemplary competition procedure, leading to the selection of the best projects in a very short time. These projects were the Civic Centre of the Isola-Garibaldi district, the Padiglione per l'infanzia (Children's pavilion) in the Integrated Garibaldi-Repubblica Intervention Plan, and the Cavalcavia Bussa elevated walkway. The excellent results gained from this experience have led to the method being adopted for a design competition for the remodelling of the Piazza della Scala. In future, it will be used for a series of other works promoted by the Municipality of Milan.

This concrete example demonstrates that, even within an extremely complex framework of standards and regulations, it is possible to identify procedures able to promote project quality while awaiting essential and undeferrable replacement of legislation concerning public works.

It is to be hoped that we will soon be able to rely on clear, flexible, comprehensible and transparent regulations that give the appropriate right of choice to public administrators for small projects, but at the same time, impose invitation contests for medium and large-scale works. When simply considering the advantages for the country, if each one of the over eight thousand Italian municipalities were able to announce at least one call for bids during its five year term in office, that would signify an average of over 1,500 calls for bids per year, instead of the current one hundred per year, it is easy to understand the cumbersome and chaotic nature of the whole regulatory system in relation to private construction projects.

The complexity of the regulatory system, inefficient control systems, overall lack of attention paid to intervention quality, lack of certainty for timeframes, rights and privileges form a particular aspect of the Italian building regulation system that in recent years has become even more complicated following an illogical legislative decentralisation process determined by the reform of Title V of the Constitution.

With the "Unblock Italy Decree" (Decreto Sblocca Italia), the government approval of a specific measure to set up a Building Regulations model on a national scale should lead to beginning the standardisation process in autumn. This standardisation is based on quality and performance characteristics adopted by more than eight thousand Italian municipalities, and could be a first important clarification and simplification process forming concrete help for a productive sector that has been undergoing a painful period for a long time.

Although encompassed in a general instrument (such as award merit in the case of project design competitions launched by private bodies, or interventions based on energy and environmental redevelopment foreseen by the Municipality of Milan, or in good practice for local regulations in a survey advertised by the monitoring body set up by Legambiente), in a similar way, certain innovative procedures relative to administrative simplification and facilitating volumetric transfer and intended use changes must form the fundamental instruments for establishing architectural and construction quality with economic and environmental sustainability in every intervention.

Of course, it must also be kept in mind that since the beginning of the crisis, about eight hundred thousand jobs have been lost by companies, tradesmen and professions in the construction industry showing the worst performance among all the Italian productive sectors, and none of the recent governments have identified an efficient support policy for the construction sector.

Therefore it is obvious that apart from the macroeconomic reasons for the crisis, and even considering the particular aspects of a sector that despite many factors of excellence, must certainly invest far more in production process innovation, it remains fundamental that every customer, whether private or public, must equip himself with a strategic vision for the future.

In this sense, the administrative, entrepreneurial, and professional experts must acquire the capacity to interpret the transformations underway in order to work towards building a political, economic, social and cultural future able to create new possibilities for growth and development.

Therefore, the challenge that awaits the government and local administrations is to create the conditions so that the many resources and expertise in our country can continue to contribute constructively to create a different and, if possible, better future.

The recent events concerning the transformation of Milan demonstrate that, if managed with competence, awareness and enthusiasm, in many cases this is still possible.

*Professional Architect, National Advisor, President of the Department of Culture, Promotion and Communications of the National Board of Architects, Town Planners, Landscape Architects and Conservationists

New Prada Foundation
headquarters in Milan,
architectural project by OMA
Photo: Bas Princen 2015,
courtesy of the Prada Foundation

Maria Vittoria Capitanucci

Is Milan travelling toward the future?

That which, in the previous editions of this series of books dedicated to contemporary Milan, could be a reflection on the possible future of the city in view of Expo, also in light of the various changes that have affected the Lombard capital over the last decade — such as the series of great master plans whose success and results were still open to interpretation —, today has become a real condition, almost completely consolidated, which has triggered new fronts and prospects. At times they are unexpected in a city that, while remaining anchored to its administrative and institutional limit, is now clearly experiencing a regional dimension, if not an inter-regional one as well. In this sense, the occasion of Expo led to two seemingly antithetical effects: on the one hand a strong push toward surpassing the concept itself of the city (including the wide-spread one) going, as we said, well beyond the urban and metropolitan definition, and on the other, focussing on specific elements of the city's "historic" fabric, on the redevelopment and reuse of monuments and "tall" features. This included a focus on a series of realities in the urban fabric that were never resolved, almost ghost places, also made up of abandoned, long forgotten, or interstitial areas. In this regard, see the very interesting work that the Politecnico di Milano has been heading up since 2013 (in association with a number of international universities) with the Project Ri-formare Milano, a teaching and research initiative sponsored by the School of Architecture and the Politecnico in collaboration with the Department for Urban Planning, Private Building, Agriculture of the Municipality of Milan. Coordinated by the School's Presidency and a number of very able and enthusiastic teachers (including Ilaria Valente, Corina Morandi, Paolo Mazzoleni, Barbara Cappetti), this project, now in its second phase, has identified a new series of areas in states of degradation and abandonment. These have garnered interest and become the objects of analysis and planning for some courses. The intent is not only to do a mapping, but above all to reconstruct scenarios, to propose the redevelopment of entire urban systems. While waiting to reinterpret the results of these directions also through a series of videos and a film made by the Centro Sperimentale di Cinematografia (Experimental Centre of Cinematography, partner for the occasion), drawing attention to this urban condition can certainly be considered a turning point and moment of awareness triggered by the long-awaited Expo. In any case, what seemed to be a decade of patchy growth, where the absence of a general program foreshadowed the worst in a transformation of the city that was perhaps too risky, indeed, under the circumstances, with an administration which managed to seize and control a weighty and unrestrained legacy, triggered by previous choices and regulatory failures as well as economic interests that went far beyond individual

MUDEC Museo delle Culture
(Museum of Culture)
Sinuous internal courtyard
of the museum: ceiling detail
© Photo OskarDaRiz

choices and policies, seems to have been resolved through a form of reconciliation with the city itself. Those that appeared to be new grafts, not without their interesting features but far too highly touted, were well metabolized by opening up to new urban visions. Given this positive interpretation of the new Milan, certainly we cannot postpone the long delays that have seen project players who could have been of great quality such as David Chipperfield for the Ansaldo Città delle culture (City of Cultures, now Mudec). His project ended in controversy arising from a series of complications and irregularities in the construction details and the fitting of the materials, to the point of inducing the well-known British architect, in Italy also to work on the Justice Citadel in Salerno, to not acknowledge the work. The very elegant construction suggests the contemporary condition, the conversion of a former industrial area but also fragmentation and re-composition. It skilfully brings into play spaces with great quality, some pre-existing and others new, situated around a sinuous courtyard. All of this is in what was once the historic city outskirts. Today, it has been turned into one of the main districts for the world of design on the occasion of the famous international event, and is one of the areas in the southwest part of the city that has undergone numerous interventions. Rethought also in functional terms the beautiful museum, a translucent and multifunctional lantern for this part of Milan, was recently inaugurated, twelve years after the tender.

The other star that has been slow to shine is certainly the new home of the Feltrinelli Foundation, but not because of the project's quality. It was designed by Swiss architects Herzog & de Meuron, points of reference in contemporary architecture. For the first time, they are at long last working in the Milan area with a project that "takes charge" of an "open" area in the city centre, between the monumental cemetery and Garibaldi station. Various vicissitudes, also linked to a series of misunderstandings with the superintendents, have lengthened the construction time of this metropolitan "shed". Work began in 2011, and eventually will be built in an area "whose final destiny" was that of a plant nursery, adjacent to the great transformations taking place in the Garibaldi/Porta Nuova area. Events have also led to downsizing the project from its initial dimension, in which a double body was planned for Piazzale Baiamonti, providing a counterpoint and background to the two historic toll gates. Work for the third "cultural" project has been less dramatic. The great fashion giant Prada commissioned Rem Koolhaas and OMA to build the new Foundation headquarters in a former industrial area on the outskirts of the historic south-east side of the city. The site sits between restored sheds and warehouses that are still used, very close to the area's main throughway, Corso Lodi. Here, along the wall that marks the former distillery, is a turreted element, with a folded and protruding front, indicating the presence of the new complex. It consists of independent reclaimed buildings, galleries, which have maintained their pre-existing distinctive features, all revolving around the "Podium", the central element, the "Ideal Museum", a large and imposing rectangular gallery, porous and dark, that forms an ideal connection with all other functions. At this point, it raises the question of how the Foundation's presence will be capable of inspiring new relationships and redeveloping the area already affected by a constellation of "presences" that still have not become interconnected. Certainly it will not be as easy as the situation in the Risorgimento/Piave area, which has undergone a significant revitalization implemented, perhaps unknowingly, by a succession of episodic projects scattered throughout the district by the famous brand Dolce & Gabbana: a series of "restorations" and new structures with a sophisticated impact and quality, designed by the studio Piuarch. These triggered, although it was not a premeditated urban planning action, the "rejuvenation" and re-functionalization of what was a quiet residential bourgeois area close to the historical centre. Yet in terms of places for culture, there are great expectations for the new campus of the University Bocconi under the banner of the studio Sanaa, Kazuyo Sejima and Ryue Nishizawa, whose works, finally, just began recently. Planned for an area of 35,000 square metres, once occupied by Milan's principal milk processing plant, the project will begin with the university residence with places for three hundred (the tallest building) and, with it, a new walkway in the Ravizza Park will be opened between Via Sarfatti and Viale Toscana. It will reorganize the entire area of the well-known Milanese university and the city. The acclaimed Japanese studio had to redesign the project with which it won the international competition in 2012, making adjustments to the high rise and lowering it from 15 to 10 floors. It also had to provide a functional redevelopment and landscaping of public municipal areas, as indicated by the planning commission in 2014, which feared an enclave type of enclosure in the new university complex. By 2019, the area between Via Castelbarco, Viale Toscana, Via Bocconi and Via Sarfatti, will have the residential tower, a sports area with an Olympic pool of 50 metres, the headquarters of the Business School of the University and recreation areas for students. This project should also interact, in the same area, with the previously restored Officine Meccaniche (OM), surrounded by the memories of the industrial park, marked by the presence of towers designed by Massimiliano Fuksas and residential courtyard buildings by Valentino Benati. In the same way, plans underway for the Milanofiori Nord area, according to the masterplan in terms of flow activation and the reorganization of regional relationships, should be recognized as interesting. This is the case with the former Alfa Romeo at Portello, for example. After the quality of the architecture by Valle, Zucchi and Canali, it has also given the city a new square with Emilio Isgrò's urban artwork and the flooring by Topotek. It finally interacts with its surroundings despite the deep ruptures in the road that characterized the limits, partly also surpassed by a walkway suspended between the new park and the area of the square and the former Fiera di Milano. The Milanofiori north area, with the master plan by the Dutch Van Egeraat, continues the "socialization" adventure with the territory, offering a quite unique glimpse of architectural quality (the residential crescent of OBR, the ABDA subsidized housing, the sinuous office building CZA and the Nestlé headquarters of Park Associati) finally connected to the commercial system of the 5+1, to the same Assago and the highway infrastructure system that has become the landscape and background. Porta Nuova/Isola/Varesine finally opens its complex system of greenery to the relationship between the parties and the rest of the territory. Above all, it shifts

Feltrinelli Foundation at Porta Volta, project by Herzog & De Meuron

Le residenze La Corte Verde di Corso Como, designed by studio CZA Cino Zucchi Architetti, in the Porta Nuova quarter

the epicentre of its major "urban" contribution to the Varesine area, putting it in direct relation with Piazzale Principessa Clotilde/ Corso di Porta Nuova/Via Filzi/Piazza Repubblica. A long dormant cul de sac that lacerated an area only apparently connected and strongly limited by the crossing of Via Melchiorre Gioia, now overcome by the intelligent connection created by the overhead pedestrian bridge. This is also happening with City Life, where the reorganization of the park's green and the beginning of the end of construction is opening new perspectives up to the city, and the neighbourhoods. The presence of the very remarkable Torre Allianz by Arata Isozaki, visible yet never intrusive, subtle and discreet as it is, inspired in part by the Pirelli skyscraper, certainly has had and will have a leading role in the city skyline; in each case it is necessary to understand the extent to which the other two towers (one by Daniel Libeskind and the other by Zaha Hadid), will reduce the appeal or interact with the group thanks to the definition of the internal piazza designed by One Works. Certainly, also, the system of the park green that had crept between the various constructions opened a historically fenced area to its surroundings, an effect also understood by one of the most austere "botanical" associations in Milan, Orticola, which recently signed an agreement with City Life for the management of a special "green" area inside the park for their initiatives and events. Thinking back to the residential aspect envisaged in this master plan, "bastions" on the extreme borders of the area, it should be noted that a theme perhaps unjustly "set aside" in this publication has been that of housing. Not only for reasons of space, the city continues to produce and reproduce, but for its ability to trigger new relationships in the area with respect to other types, so except in a few territorially far-reaching cases (ABDA in Assago, MCA architects and Teknoarch in Cascina Merlata), there has been no return, as in previous volumes, to the "prodigious" and very remarkable cases of the subsidized housing of Abitare Milano (Mab in Via Gallarate, Cecchi and Lima in Via Ovada, Consalez and Rossi in Via Civitavecchia, Oda Associati in Via Senigaglia). Nor have the super-luxury towers and condominiums which were a part of the initial stage been taken up again; those from the first perhaps exasperated phase of renewal, following a previous political and economic push, buildings that are now outdated. The city, rather, is now finding its expression with a constellation of contained construction projects designed to fill the empty abandoned spaces, or to replace the previous "anonymous" buildings or those that are no longer "sustainable". We are talking about the cases of the former Enel offices in Porta Volta, now residences with overhanging verandas, designed by the studio De Architettura, which also designed the imposing tower in the Maciachini area; and the two condominiums by Marzio Rusconi Clerici in Via Cola di Rienzo (with Giorgio Merico) and Via Altaguardia (this with Agnoletto); and the studio Beretta Associati working simultaneously on Via Nievo — in the area of the unforgettable former residence for the elderly of the Jewish community of Depas, D'Urbino, Lomazzi —, the large residential project in via Piranesi and, more recently, its role in the redevelopment of a huge property of Cassa Depositi e Prestiti in Via Montello. Not to mention Cecchi & Lima working in the heart of Milan's ancient Roman quarter on the project for residential buildings and public spaces, or the sophisticated studio De Amicis Architetti, with the sundial courtyard residence in Via Canonica and the dual system of Zucchi's "green courts" in Porta Nuova. They push with undeniable architectural quality toward a common and contained direction reassuring modernity and especially a "densification" of the urban fabric without serious disruption to the fabric and the relationship with pre-existing architecture. In this sense, in the heart of Milan, remains the significant and even unexpected case of the Litta residences by AMDL-Michele de Lucchi, where we can trace the desire to rebuild the relationship between places, parts and elements of the city in a luxury setting in one of the monuments of seventeenth-century Milan. Finally, an inevitable reflection on the fate and condition of the Expo Area. This is certainly a rare and important event — perhaps more than might have been imagined by many of us who consider this type of event as outdated as well as conceptually and ethically obsolete — an opportunity that has demonstrated up to now (although with undue delays now physiologically inherent to the DNA of our country) to have triggered many changes, not least for giving a programmatic and significant boost to situations that have long been bogged down, for example in terms of infrastructure policies, relations with the territory, and naturally in relation to opportunities related to the specific cases of linguistic and technological experimentation and in terms of sustainability. Reassuring forecasts for a future destination for a university campus (apparently the agreement is now signed) and news (biased?) that some of the pavilions will be kept — and here we can only hope for the maintenance of the Slow food pavilion by Herzog & de Meuron — but also the pavilions of Chile, China, Brazil as well as the sinuous pavilion 0 by aMDL, Michele De Lucchi, almost a work of land art and perhaps one of the symbolic buildings of this Expo. And finally, last but not least, there is the sophisticated and intelligent system of the clusters, collective in the sense of their function but also in terms of design, the result of the Politecnico's involvement with the most interesting universities and international design schools. While waiting for clarification on the final destination and rapports on an urban scale between the Expo area and its structures, we could look at a possible temporary use for the pavilions that many nations are offering free for cultural events related to the world of design, as was proposed by the Triennale of Milan but also others. In each case the Expo 2010 company had declared itself ready to work with Milan to study the conversion of the Rho-Pero from 2011, making its expertise available; now it is necessary to understand how the different social, entrepreneurial, and technical forces and investors will react, forces that came into play in the meantime and, above all, whether the idea of a real public design competition might be feasible for the urban and architectural renewal of the Expo Area. We wait and in the meantime, the city goes on changing.

*Historian and architecture critic, she graduated from the Polytechnic of Milan and received her Doctorate in the History and Criticism of Architecture at the University Federico II of Naples. She teaches History of Contemporary Architecture at the School of Architecture, Politecnico di Milano, contributes to numerous specialized publications and is the author of monographs and essays.

Milano Centre

1. Expo Gate
Via Luca Beltrami

2. Atelier Castello
Piazza Castello

3. Triennale Terrace Restaurant
Viale Alemagna

4. Litta Residences
Corso Magenta, Via Illica

5. Priceless Restaurant Milan
Piazza della Scala

6. Redevelopment of the Ospedale Maggiore Policlinico, Mangiagalli and Regina Elena hospital complex
Via Francesco Sforza

7. Redevelopment of the Centro Balneare Caimi
Via Carlo Botta

8. Residential apartment building
Viale Monte Grappa

9. Hotel Duca d'Aosta
Piazza Duca d'Aosta

10. Excelsior Hotel Gallia
Piazza Duca d'Aosta

11. Porta Nuova Garibaldi

12. UniCredit Pavilion
Porta Nuova

13. E3_East Office Building
Porta Nuova

14. Porta Nuova Varesine

15. Gioiaotto
Via Melchiorre Gioia

16. Porta Nuova Isola

17. V33 Residential apartment building
Via Volturno

18. Istituto Gonzaga
Via Vitruvio / Via Settembrini

19. City Pavilion
Piazza Duca d'Aosta

1 Expo Gate
Via Luca Beltrami

Scandurra Studio Architettura

The two Expo Gate pavilions occupy the whole length of Via Beltrami and frame a plain open central space. This open space concept, echoed in the pavilions themselves, has set the scene for the events and preparations linked with Expo 2015 and will continue throughout the period of the fair. The lightweight, transparent, modular pavilions act as a backdrop to the activities organised, strongly showcasing the events without overshadowing the content. Because of their location and design, the Expo gates designed by the Scandurra Studio, have a great communicative impact. Expo Gate is positioned on the main artery that leads through the city centre from the Duomo as far as the Arco della Pace on the same trajectory as corso Sempione, passing through the Loggia dei Mercanti, the Palazzo della Ragione, Via Dante and Castello Sforzesco.

The structure is based on an expression of lightness and was built using basic technology. It is composed of strong metal frames, arc-welded together. The Milan Expo 2015 infopoint is a complex system composed of simple elements. The layout is neutral and flexible like the exterior that can be easily modified according to necessity.
C.G.

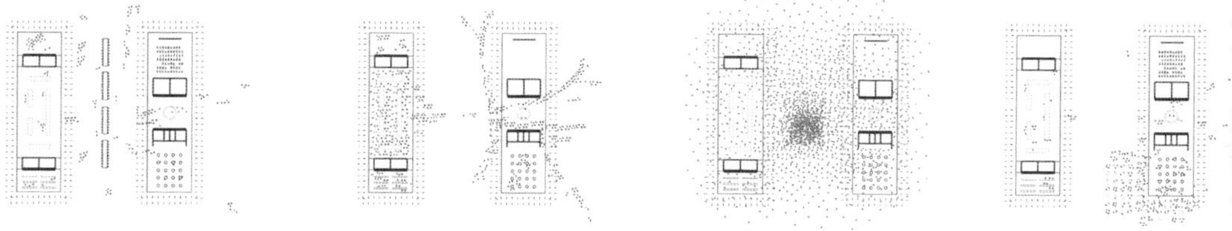

Outline of structure applications and uses: events, exhibitions, opening, and view on a sunny day

View of Expo Gate from Piazza Castello

Front view of the structure

Expo Gate interior

2 **Atelier Castello**
Piazza Castello

Guidarini & Salvadeo + Snark

#nevicata14 is the winning design from the consultation (which involved eleven architectural firms) proposed by the Milan Triennale and accepted by the City to temporarily equip Piazza Castello for the period during Expo. This special design proposal included a number of "players" — architects, engineers, administrators, intellectuals, but also ordinary citizens — and involves setting up the open space in front of the Castello Sforzesco with equipment for public use. Therefore seating, structures to shade people from the sun, cool mist dispensers, platforms for public activities or entertainment, new lighting equipment, signal poles and a wi-fi network are all part of a flooring designed as a series of signs. These elements facilitate the creation of a rest area and participation in collective activities, following a concept that emphasizes the pedestrian area, seen as the ideal extension of Sempione Park to beyond the Castle, to the boundary with Foro Buonaparte. The project, in fact, also includes the installation of removable potted trees, grouped to form small gardens, and which can function as true green areas that give shade. All devices and trees are organized in relation to the presence of the white areas. These are circular and of various sizes, traced on the ground, like large patches of snow during the thaw. *#nevicata14* is totally reversible.
G.P.

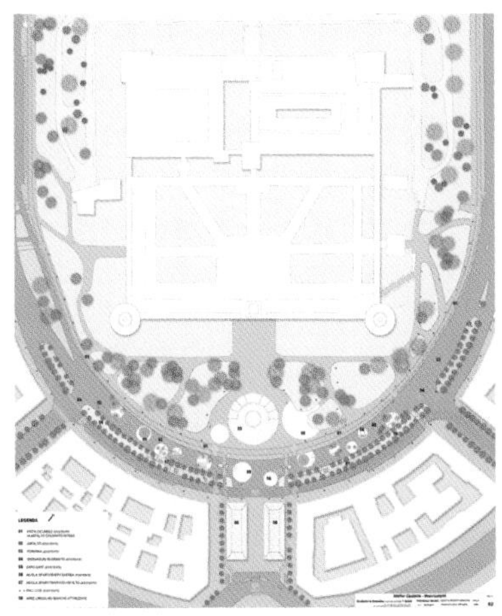

Intervention plan

Project image *#nevicata 14*

View of the piazza with seating and urban decor elements

3 **Triennale Terrace Restaurant**
Viale Alemagna

OBR

With its long history in promoting architectural research, the Milan Triennale has launched a series of initiatives to coincide with Expo 2015 and with the 2016 event, when it will host the new International Exhibition.

In 2015, the new Terrazza restaurant designed by studio OBR (Paolo Brescia and Tommaso Principi) will be erected on the roof of the Palazzo dell'Arte along with the Arts and Foods Pavilion curated by Germano Celant, and staged by the Italo Rota Studio.

The Milan Triennale has launched the restoration of its panoramic roof terrace faithful to the original design by Giovanni Muzio, and will offer the public a new top quality restaurant. The new temporary restaurant, winner of the design contest, is based on the concept of a small greenhouse immersed in the green shade of a scenographic awning. The design features a warm elegant atmosphere with a unique view over the park and the skyline of the city.

The greenhouse — measuring 33 x 5 metres, and 3 metres high — is recessed in relation to the terrace portico, and is composed of a slim modular metal structure that can be easily assembled on site. The Pavilion recalls the proportions of the seven arch spans of the Palazzo dell'Arte design by Muzio.

Visitors will be able to enjoy a large open space surrounded by planters filled with flowers, aromatic herbs and seasonal vegetables. A small informal exhibition area will be set up under the existing projecting roof.

The awning symbolises the temporary ephemeral nature of the restaurant; during the day it provides shade over the greenhouse structure, and at night lights and images linked with themes and events promoted by the Triennale at Expo will be projected on the awning screen.

During the Expo event, the small temporary pavilion on the terrace will exhibit examples of haute cuisine and design, suspended between the park, the city and the sky.

A.M.

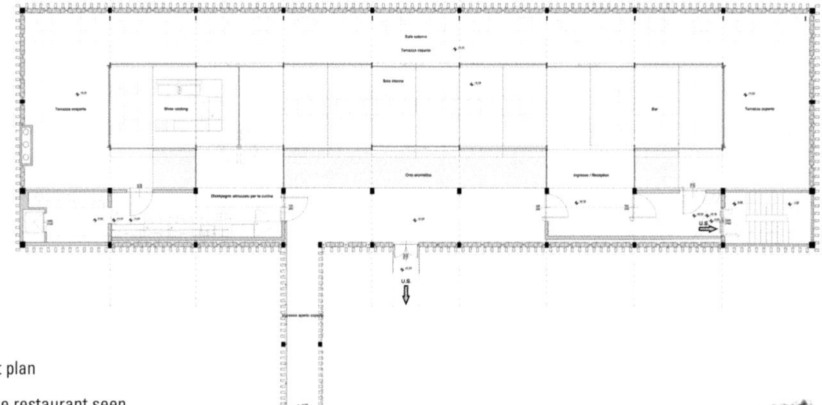

Restaurant plan

The Terrace restaurant seen from the Parco del Sempione

Completely glassed-in restaurant interior

The vegetable-herb garden recalls the principal themes linked with Expo and the excellence of Italian Haute Cuisine

4 **Litta Residences**

Corso Magenta, Via Illica

aMDL architect Michele De Lucchi,
head architect Giovanna Latis

A wide-ranging intervention in the heart of the city. This residential complex has revitalised a monumental area significantly marked by the presence of the historic Litta building, overlooking Corso Magenta. It consists of a complex of buildings and courtyards located between Corso Magenta and the Foro Bonaparte.

The theme of courtyards, designed to create private internal pathways, becomes a generating element for the project, enhancing public spaces and adding to the historical courtyards (Cortile d'Onore, dell'Orologio and della Cavallerizza), giving the city two new courtyards, Cortile Foro Bonaparte and Cortile Brentano. Alongside this complex, the green landscaping connects the historic garden with new private green areas and residential buildings.

The program is shared with the Lombardy Regional Directorate for Cultural Heritage and Landscape (Direzione Regionale per i Beni Culturali e Paesaggistici della Lombardia), which in regard to this, has drawn up a declaration of cultural interest, indicating the methods to be used in approaching the changes underway.

The project consists of three buildings, named A, B and C, which are accessible from Corso Magenta, Via Illica and Via Brentano.

Building A, not yet constructed, should take the place of a post-war building of little architectural value with five floors above ground and two floors below ground to be used for parking.

Here, in the structural lattice seen on the façade and the geometric simplicity of the volume, we find the most cultivated Lombard architectural tradition, going from the rationalism of Terragni and Gardella, to the "classicism" of Muzio and Cassi Ramelli.

This building forms the boundary of the west side of the Litta Garden, also subject to redefinition, bounded on the opposite side by the so-called building B, also open onto the cortile Foro Bonaparte.

For building B, nineteenth-century, as well as for building C, the restoration and conservation project aims at maintaining the original volumes and prospects, but from the perspective of a functional redistribution that enables its new residential role.

Building B is spread over four floors, divided into two spacious housing units per floor, in continuity with the tradition of this bourgeois residential area of the city. The recovery of the attic has made the enhancement of the top floor possible, with the creation of spacious apartments on two levels.

The building group C, consisting of a series of buildings that are each very different from the other, for their period of construction and architectural style, runs along the Cortile Foro Bonaparte and turns the corner to create the Cortile Brentano, a small courtyard with railing that provides the charm of "old Milan".

Here, the work on the buildings was meticulous and respectful of the different types of architecture, aimed at creating twenty-four residential units on different levels, often lofts, with private gardens and new overhanging galleries. The galleries or loggias, the third important theme of the monumental part of Palazzo Litta, after the courtyards and gardens, become the element of modernity and quality, designed to bring quality of living to the environment.

Below the Cortile Foro Bonaparte are two floors of underground parking, with access from Via Illica. Its con struction also led to the discovery of some Roman artifacts.

A.D.

Project sketch of Building A of new realization

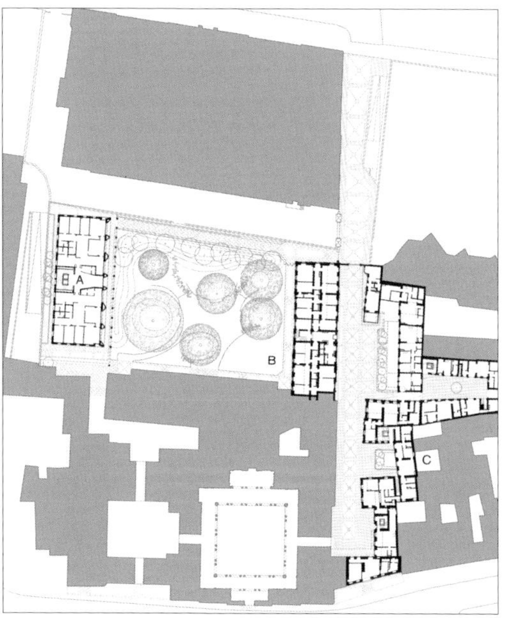

The Cortile Foro Buonaparte, a private street that connects Corso Magenta and Foro Buonaparte.
View of one of the internal courtyards

General layout of the intervention showing the buildings, garden, and courtyards

Reinforcing of the walkway galleries in the Brentani courtyards

Facade restoration in the Cortile Foro Buonaparte

5 **Priceless Restaurant Milan**

Piazza della Scala

Park Associati

The Priceless Restaurant in Milan is a fleeting temporary installation; a module designed to be transferred and placed on top of existing buildings in high visibility locations. Set up as a restaurant, but also for other events, the pavilion is currently located on the roof of Palazzo Beltrami, in Piazza della Scala.

This event was sponsored by MasterCard Europe as part of the "Priceless Cities" initiative — a vast tourist promotion program set up in large international cities, and managed by the 4Ward company, while the Banca Intesa San Paolo collaborated to provide a location of excellence, the historical Palazzo Beltrami, which hosts the contemporary and modern art collections belonging to the former Banca Commerciale Italiana, also on show in the adjacent buildings, Palazzo Anguissola and Palazzo Brentani.

This event follows the previous experience of the travelling restaurant in 2012-13 with the pop-up structure called the Cube which sat overlooking the Piazza del Duomo; it was designed by the Milanese architectural and design firm, Park Associati, and commissioned by the Belgian agency, Absolute Blue. The concept was resumed and developed for the Milan Expo 2015 for the program: "Expo in the city".

The restaurant is designed as a kind of 'mobile gastronomical theatre' where international celebrity chefs are invited to perform in rotation, with show cooking demonstrations for guest diners. The architectural design of the pavilion by Park Associati is a complex structure with strong but not overpowering impact, in arresting but not discordant contrast with the surrounding buildings, thanks to the regular geometrical form of the main glass structure that hovers like a wide screen over the historical city centre, protected by irregular gilded "wings" in slatted sheet metal.

A contemporary spider poised in the midst of history. Inside, a single table hosts twenty-four diners who share a unique experience; if necessary, the kitchen area can be isolated from the dining area by sliding partitions. The table can be raised to the ceiling to leave the internal space completely free. The two long sides of the dining area are composed of floor to ceiling French windows that provide access to the out-door roof terrace with its breath-taking views.

The Milan Priceless Restaurant is not limited to simply hosting the restaurant space: every week interviews and talks will be held on different topics and subjects in line with the Milan Expo 2015 theme: "Feed the Planet, Energy for life".

A.M.

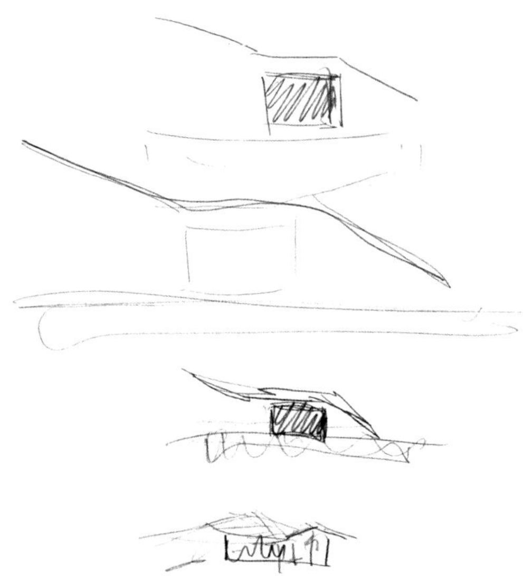

View of the temporary structure integrated within the urban context

Study sketch of the Priceless Pavilion

The Priceless Pavilion, placed on the roof of Palazzo Beltrami, headquarters of the Banca Intesa Sanpaolo in Piazza della Scala

following pages
Nocturnal view of the terrace

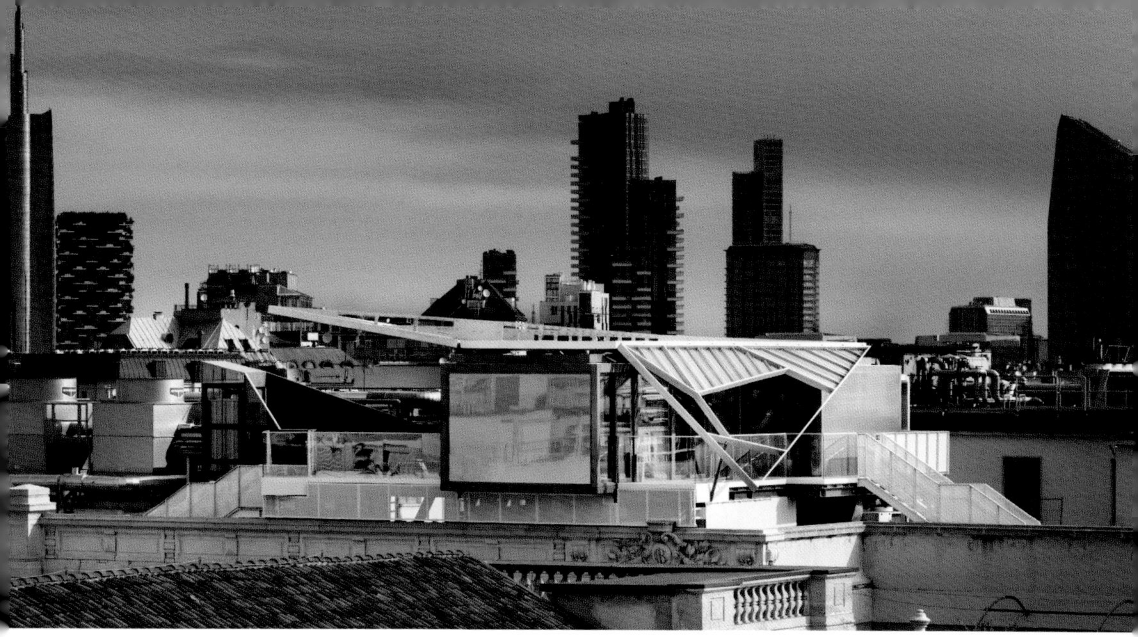

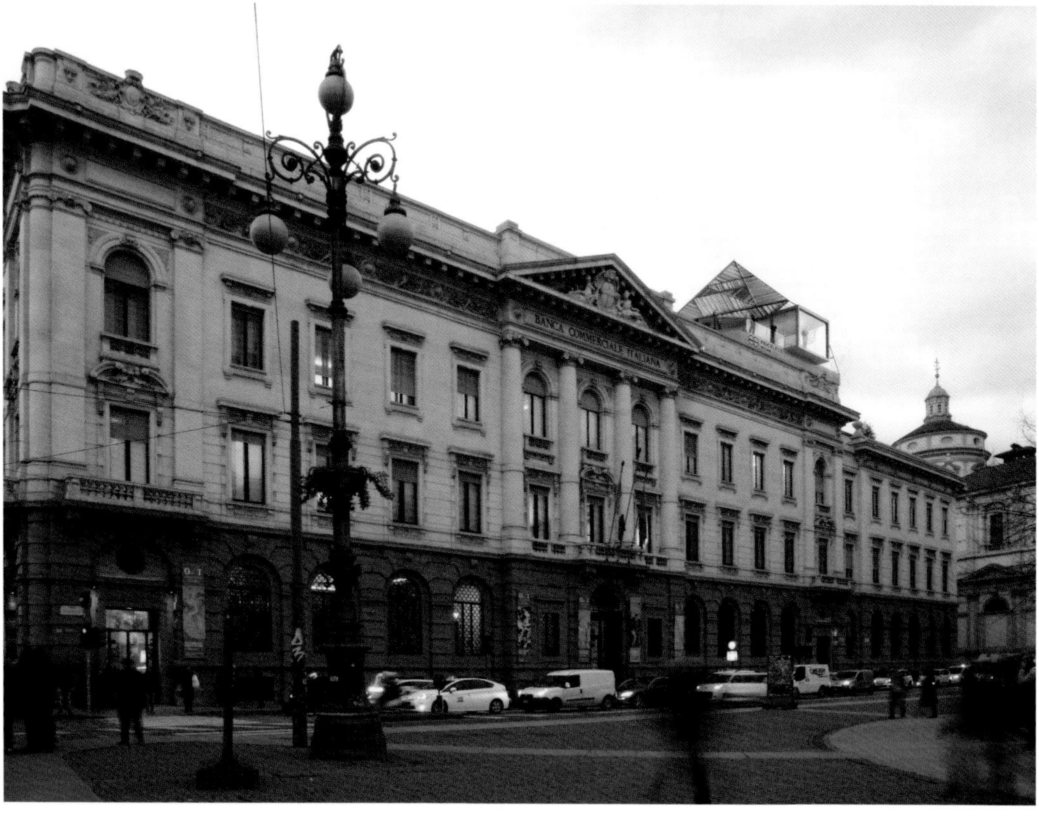
BANCA COMMERCIALE ITALIANA

6 Redevelopment of the Ospedale Maggiore Policlinico, Mangiagalli and Regina Elena hospital complex

Via Francesco Sforza

Central Building and Torre Sforza: Boeri Studio (Stefano Boeri, Gianandrea Barreca, Giovanni La Varra) / Barreca & La Varra, Stefano Boeri

Mortuary and Logistics: ABDArchitetti, C+S Architects

The Ospedale Maggiore in Milan, traditionally known as Ca' Granda, was founded in 1456 by the Duke Francesco Sforza and designed by the famous architect, Antonio Averlino, known as Filarete. At the beginning of the twentieth century the main hospital complex was transferred a short distance from the original site to its current location, a large area enclosed by Via Francesco Sforza, corso di Porta Romana, Via Lamarmora and Via Commenda, where numerous buildings were constructed over the years for various departments.

An international competition was launched in 2007 to select a project for intervention on the inadequate current structure composed of an enclosure and a large number of pavilions. It was designed to generate new contemporary functions and consistency within an integrated project design concept. The core of the project, the new hospital structure called Central Building, connects its network of medical and alternative services with the other pavilions. This link-up is one of the most important aspects of the program that also includes a protected medical transit circuit at a height of 12.80 metres, above which is a second open-air level, at a height of 16.30 metres, leading to the roof garden on the Policlinico central building.

The Central Building is composed of two linear constructions, the north and south wings (Stecca Nord and Stecca Sud) 28 metres high, that form the northern and southern boundaries of the area, connected to each other by a central block, 18.25 metres high, covered with a roof garden.

The North and South blocks are based on a five-section model with a central double corridor, and the second to sixth floors are mainly destined for recovery rooms. The lower floors are divided into various sections including recovery rooms, consultation rooms, emergency, and intensive care. Separating the North and South blocks from the central building are patios of various sizes. The "mirrored" structure of the complex was chosen because of the need to maintain two existing buildings that created certain limits for the new project design: the Litta pavilion to the north and the church and dormitory block to the south. This complex also includes the Sforza Tower, destined for activities complementary to hospital functions.

A tunnel passes under Via della Commenda, to link the various blocks and connect the logistics centre with the Central Building basement; it acts as a distribution network for the whole pavilion system.

The second intervention stage will include a structure called Polo di Piazza Umanitaria, which will house the mortuary, autopsy room, and a range of logistics functions.

Developed by a design team, ABDArchitetti and C+S Architects, working in temporary association, this new pavilion will house the mortuary and is designed to coordinate the internal-external flow of the existing structures through the traditional linear building structure. It features unexpected elements and projections that separate the various spaces of the hospital complex with strict, clean lines and refined materials.

This international competition-winning project designed to cater for funeral services, features clean sober lines echoed in the solid construction materials — white stone and glass — while harmonising with its urban surroundings. The mortuary, a compact white structure, is not concealed within the hospital complex, but forms the fourth side of the piazza, opening onto a tree-lined green space in its civic role as a "secular church". On the opposite side, the structure continues alongside the existing buildings to form a long internal courtyard that creates a protected waiting area. This contains a small garden with a long reflecting pool mirrored in the large windows on the southern facade.

As well as providing innovative structures with efficient and coordinated buildings and circuits, the redevelopment project also includes over 5 acres of public green space.

M.G.M./M.T.

The Central Building features a roof garden

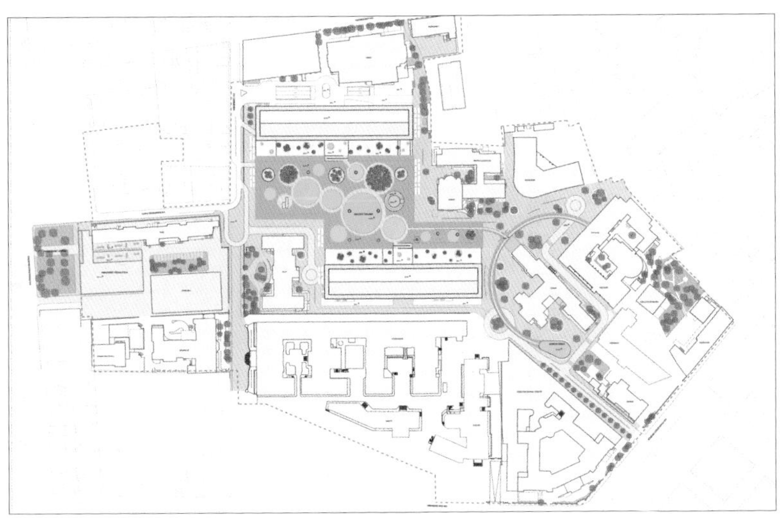

General layout

The small internal garden at the Mortuary, project by ABDArchitetti and C+S Architects

Northern facade (above) and southern facade of the Mortuary

The compact white structure of the Mortuary faces a tree-lined square and forms the fourth facade of the complex

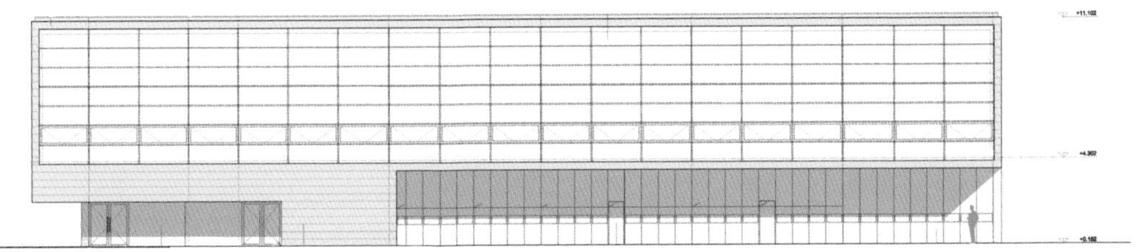
+11.102
+4.302
+0.162

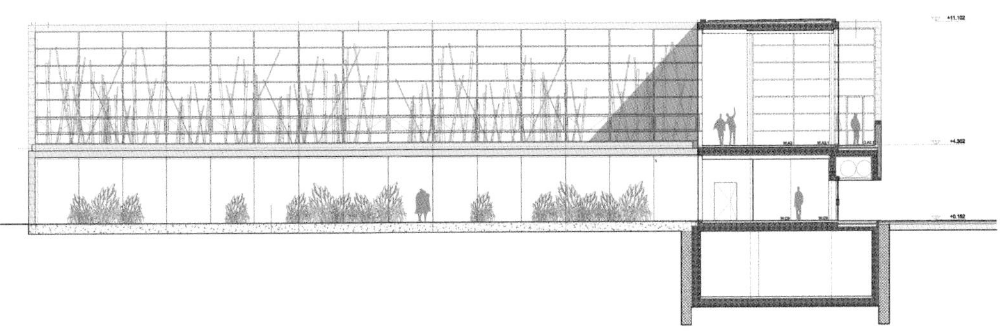
+11.102
+4.302
+0.162

7 **Redevelopment of the Centro Balneare Caimi**
Via Carlo Botta

Giovanna Latis, Elena Martucci, Laboratorio Permanente – Nicola Russi, Angelica Sylos Labini with the artistic direction of Michele De Lucchi and Andrée Ruth Shammah

After a long and glorious past, the Centro Balneare Caimi designed by Engineer Secchi in 1939, has been subject to decades of decline and abandon. In 2013, the Fondazione Pier Lombardo agreed to bring it back to life by including it in the cultural program of the Franco Parenti Theatre, returning to the city a place of great historical value, and a multifunctional facility for sport, leisure and recreation.

Andrée Ruth Shammah, director of the theatre, called on Michele De Lucchi (responsible for the theatre renovation) to coordinate the work of three young architects for the restoration of the pool and the external areas, assigning each one with a specific task: the new theatre space, the service building, and the changing rooms.

Work on the external areas is focussed on conservative restoration and technological upgrading of all the original structures in a combined project carried out by Giovanna Latis, Elena Martucci and Nicola Russi. The two swimming pools (the 50-metre Olympic pool and the semi-circular pool) surrounded by green lawns will be used for swimming and will be equipped with mobile stages. The circulation in the external areas will be enhanced with the addition of a covered colonnade for events and performances, personally designed by Michele De Lucchi.

A new multifunctional sunken theatre space will be installed under one of the lawns. Designed by Giovanna Latis, it will have access to the ground floor through a glassed foyer opening onto the renovated Largo Franco Parenti and the pool gardens. The new space is also connected to the lower foyer of the Teatro Parenti, and is designed as a theatrical laboratory with changing configurations that can be created using mobile wooden tiers with incorporated seating arranged between the stalls and the balconies.

The small building formerly used for the changing rooms and pool services has been completely restored by Laboratorio Permanente, into an artistic and cultural centre. Each space has been restored according to a different functional plan to house exhibition spaces, areas for recreation and sport, a bar-café and restaurant. Any added elements have been strongly focused on respecting the style of the original building.

The wing destined for the changing rooms, designed by Elena Martucci, is positioned at the side of the pool and will become a flexible scenographic complex. A wooden walkway crosses the total 100-metre length and mobile partitions divide the spaces preserving the layout of the pre-existing cabins. Inside the common changing rooms, stretched fabric panels create the intimacy of individual changing rooms. When needed, the partitions and panels disappear to create a space that can be used for other activities: events, fashion shows, or theatrical performances.

The intervention aims at integrating the Teatro Franco Parenti space with the new areas of the swimming pool complex, recovering the multifunctional nature of the structure and blending the theatrical experience with areas for sport while preserving all the original architectural elements and style.
A.M.

The front of the Teatro Parenti that houses the foyer overlooking the swimming pool area

View of the redeveloped swimming pool and external areas. In the background, the facade of the ex-changing rooms building

Axonometric blow up of the internal layout of the changing rooms in the long wing of the cabins

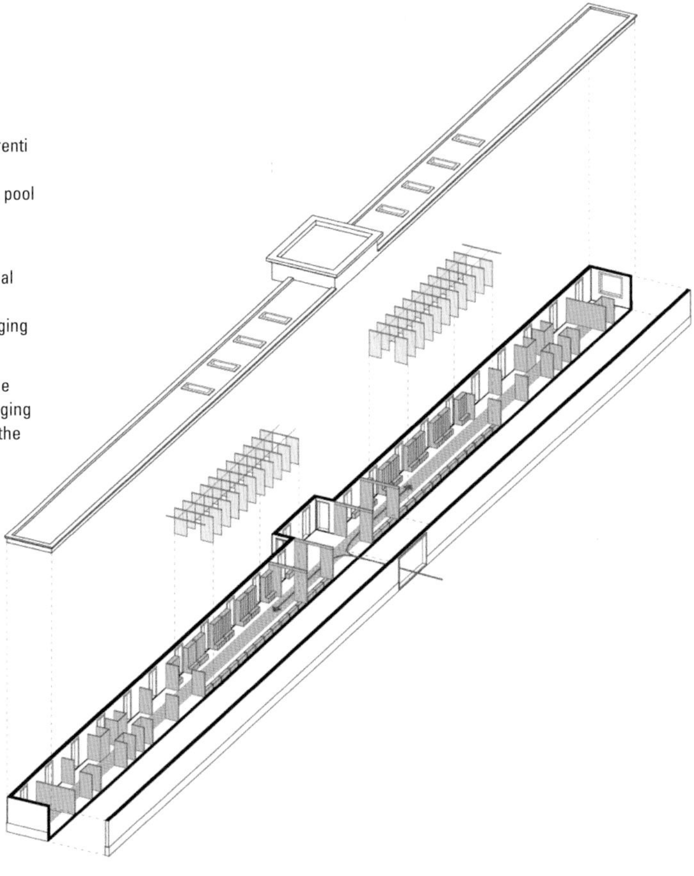

Exhibition spaces created inside the ex-changing rooms building

The access stairs from the swimming pool and from the foyer in Largo Franco Parenti

Cross section of the sunken room, swimming pool, changing rooms.
The ex-changing rooms building is in the background

8 **Residential apartment building**

Viale Monte Grappa

Westway Architects

The apartment building designed by Westway Architects has changed the face of Viale Monte Grappa. The project design was based on a new version of the facade of the original nineteenth-century construction, but which was lower than the two adjacent buildings. For this reason, the intervention was aimed at providing visual continuity in this section of the city. The size, form, and window opening features of the original building were respected on the main facade overlooking the street, with three different types of material for the horizontal divisions of the exterior: concrete ashlar for the ground floor, plaster finish for the centre section, and double glass skin on the top floor. The front facade is harmonised with the height of the adjacent buildings thanks to the alignment of the respective cornices. In fact, crowning the facade, a large cornice frames the window surface of the last two floors recessed two metres back from the street in a reinterpretation of the architectural crowning element on the adjacent buildings, and emphasised in a contemporary key.

The complex identity of the intervention is gradually revealed by the internal courtyard where the roofing defines the space on two different levels: the ground floor is roofed to enclose the shopping centre, and the platform created on the first floor provides a view of green plants from the upper floors , with two large trees planted at ground level, whose foliage extends through two elliptic openings in the roof to become part of the courtyard garden.

The layout is defined by the buildings of different heights with internal facades that feature alternating wood and stone cladding, enriched with projecting transparent balconies covered with plants. Arranged around the courtyard, nucleus of the entire structure, are 25 apartments of varying types and sizes, accessible from the balconies with glass parapets and iron railings that recall the traditional Milanese balconied row houses.

The project is representative for its ability to resolve the formal constraints caused by the historical fabric of the site, but at the same time, the apartment complex must satisfy current habitability objectives regarding energy efficiency.

From this aspect, the intervention forms a critical link between the traces of the past and the assertion of contemporary values.

M.T.

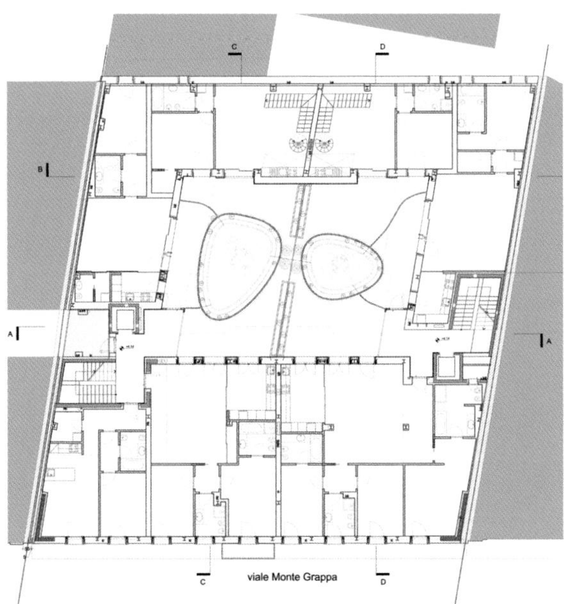

Apartment building complex plan

External facade on Viale Monte Grappa

View of internal courtyard

9 **Hotel Duca d'Aosta**

Piazza Duca d'Aosta

Onsitestudio

In Piazza Duca d'Aosta, on the corner opposite the Pirelli Tower, Onsitestudio has rejuvenated a building designed by the architect Baciocchi, instilling a new image to coincide with Expo 2015. This redevelopment project involved recreating the profile of the existing building with some demolition and reconstruction works; the accommodation capacity was been increased and improved, upgrading the energy efficiency of the whole building.

The project aimed at a concept of continuity with the existing image and with the section of the building that is to be maintained in its original state. The basic characteristics were used as inspiration for the construction of the new concept. The building will maintain its rigorous, sober and regular structure, reflecting its solid and contemporary urban image, and recalling the traditional styles and materials of Milan.

The colour and materiality associated with clinker, a material that characterised Milan in the post-war years, is linked with the pre-existing architecture. The lines of the vertical elements taper as they rise, recalling the similar structure of the Pirelli Tower. The facade echoes the depth and shadows to give the same effect as the existing building.

The whole building has been designed according to sustainability criteria using high performance technology with a holistic approach. The extremely efficient shell provides considerable energy consumption reductions. The project includes consumption control systems for air conditioning, ventilation, and hot water, all produced from renewable sources.

The atmosphere of the building is based on the memories linked with the sense of place, the repetition and regularity of the constructive elements, on certain details that are connected with the human factor, and typically traditional aspects of Milanese architecture like the portico and glossy clinker cladding on the facade.

A.M.

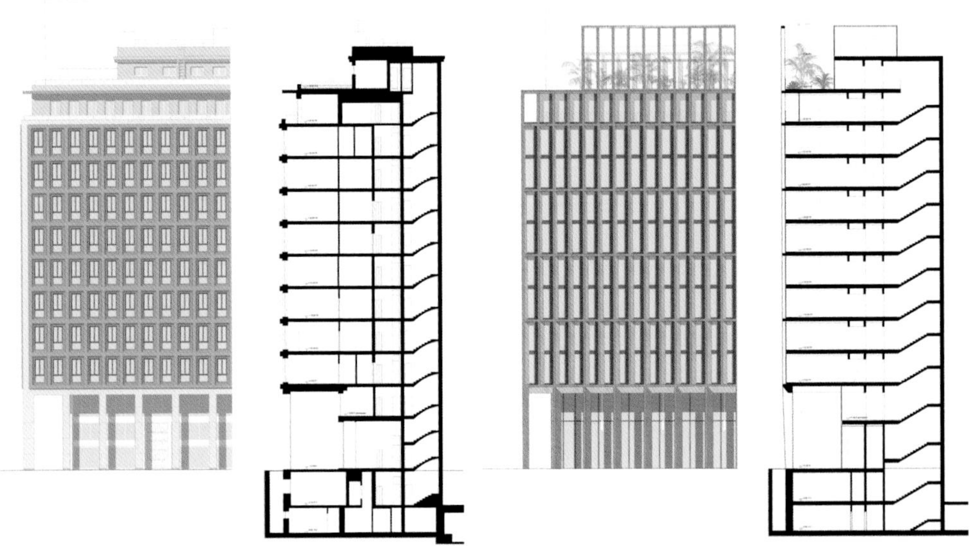

Elevations and sections of the old and new facade, project by Onsitestudio

The building's facade is composed of a single grid effect, emphasising the structure of the building with the variation in thickness of the vertical elements

View of the hotel from the piazza; on the right, the Pirelli Tower

10 **Excelsior Hotel Gallia**
Piazza Duca d'Aosta

Studio Marco Piva

The restoration and extension of the historic Excelsior Hotel Gallia in the heart of Milan is part of the wider urban redevelopment plan underway in Piazza Duca d'Aosta.

The renovation and expansion project was performed in two different stages, but coordinated together.

The first stage concerned the restoration and functional renovation of the building that dates back to the 1930s, including the complete restoration of the historic facades and the refurbishment of the existing spaces.

The new element has been developed adjacent to the historic building replacing four other structures, and will form a new morphological solution that spreads coherently along the three facades, creating an area on the ground floor that relates functionally with its surroundings and is open to create an osmotic process with the city.

The facade of the new intervention is transparent and luminous: it is composed of modules 142 centimetre wide, divided in three, with two closed panels and one openable window. The window element has an internal ledge in glass that transmits the light, recalling the traditional system on so many small balconies almost flush with the facade in dozens of historical Milanese buildings.

The interiors of the new Excelsior Hotel Gallia have been decorated with extreme care; great attention has been paid to the choice of materials, textures, and details that invoke Milan design and lifestyle, with a hint of the timeless elegance and atmosphere of Art déco.
D.S.

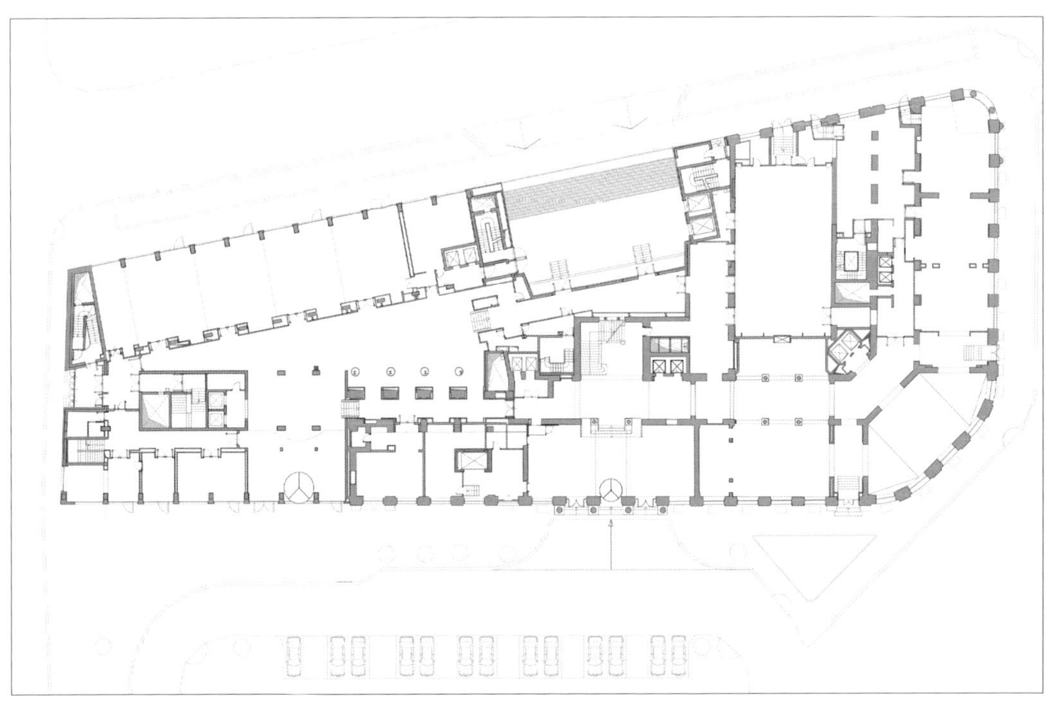

Ground floor plan
of the Hotel Excelsior Gallia

View of the Hotel Excelsior
Gallia from the Piazza
Duca d'Aosta

The new facade adjacent to
the existing historic building

11 Porta Nuova Garibaldi

Pelli Clarke Pelli Architects, Muñoz + Albin, CZA Cino Zucchi Architetti, Studio Land, Piuarch

The redevelopment of Porta Nuova Garibaldi, an area covering a surface of 290,000 square metres in the heart of Milan, recovers one of the city's most a strategic zones to form the most innovative business district of its kind in Italy, comparable to some of the most sophisticated in Europe. The integration of residential apartments, office spaces, retail stores and cultural centres, equipped to the highest technological and energy-saving standards, make Porta Nuova a multifunctional and eco-sustainable urban project unique in Italy.

The three master plans, developed by Pelli Clarke Pelli Architects, Kohn Pedersen Fox Associates and Boeri Studio, aimed at integrating and recomposing three different quarters — Brera, Isola and Repubblica — provide the area with a strong identity.

The natural continuity of the urban fabric transforms Porta Nuova Garibaldi into a gateway to the new quarter along the pedestrian ramp of Corso Como (Via Vincenzo Capelli) overlooked by top Italian and international fashion brand stores, and the Residenze di Corso Como designed by the American firm, Muñoz + Albin.

Located in Via Viganò is the residential complex, La Corte Verde di Corso Como, designed by CZA Cino Zucchi Architetti, a trapeze-shaped "porous" urban block composed of buildings of different heights and arranged around a large central garden.

The UniCredit tower is set in the new Piazza Gae Aulenti; the complex of three towers by Pelli Clarke Pelli Architects houses the UniCredit headquarters and four thousand staff members. Piazza Gae Aulenti features three circular fountains, surrounded by a 105-metre bench-sculpture in marble-concrete.

The piazza is paved with luserna stone and surrounded by two overhanging sunroofs in steel, wood and glass containing integrated solar panels, which define the public area. The piazza is 6 metres higher than the level of the city and sits at the foot of the highest building in Italy; it houses the first permanent urban art work by Alberto Garutti in Milan: twenty-three chromed brass tubes, an intervention in harmony with the architecture that surrounds it, enhancing the general impact.

The Piuarch building, that partly overlooks the central piazza, features an elegantly fluid design. The two facades are clad with contrasting systems: the side facing the piazza features large glassed walls, while the curved façade on the southern side is clad with vertical brise-soleil slatting. The five-floor building rises from the piazza to a height of thirty metres, completing the intervention and creating a link with the public section of the area. Set at a level higher than the street, it represents a strong and recognisable landmark.

The Porta Nuova Garibaldi area was the first to be completed at the end of 2012, and the complex houses some of the most important Italian and international company headquarters and brand stores, confirming the strong impact of the business district project. In 2015, the district was expanded with the UniCredit Pavilion, designed by Michele De Lucchi; another office and retail building is shortly to be constructed, designed by Mario Cucinella Architects.

A.M.

View of the buildings designed by Pelli Clarke Pelli, Unicredit headquarters

The Porta Nuova architecture has become a new landmark in Milan

The three Pelli skyscrapers
overlook Piazza Gae Aulenti

Sober fluid curves
define the urban facade
of the Piuarch building

12 **UniCredit Pavilion**
Porta Nuova

Michele De Lucchi

The multifunctional UniCredit Pavilion was designed and developed by the Michele De Lucchi architectural studio.

The project is located in a privileged position in the unique context of Porta Nuova, the meeting point of several quarters and communities of the city. This space, with its strongly versatile impact inspired by creativity, innovation and sustainability is designed for meetings, conferences, congresses, exhibitions, performances, and seminars.

With its gentle fluid lines and warm natural materials, the UniCredit Pavilion complements the strong verticality of the tall UniCredit Towers and creates a dialogue with the green park area.

Recalling an image often mentioned by the architect, De Lucchi, the UniCredit Pavilion was inspired by the form of a seed planted in the Park. As he commented: "It is immediately obvious that this is not a condominium or an office building, and it elicits the emotional strength of a monument, a symbol that connects the nature in the park with the human element in the skyscrapers".

This hybrid nature gives strength to the new space, exemplified for its wooden skeleton and glass shell, built with natural materials and modern construction techniques to give an innovative light airy atmosphere to its gentle curves.

The structure opens out to the exterior through the "wings": two large raised screen-mounted panels project news of events underway in the city. The ground floor houses a multifunctional modular auditorium; the flexible spaces, ductile applications, and adaptability for a wide range of uses make the auditorium the ideal space for hosting large events, but also different types of initiatives of various sizes. The upper section of the building houses the lounge area, a suggestive space with views that overlook the park and the city. The Art Walkway is a suspended balcony circuit arranged to host temporary exhibitions.

In addition, the building will include a kindergarten designed and developed in a functional manner in collaboration with Reggio Children following their educational project and placing strong focus on the environment, the use of ecological materials and on innovative solutions.

A.M.

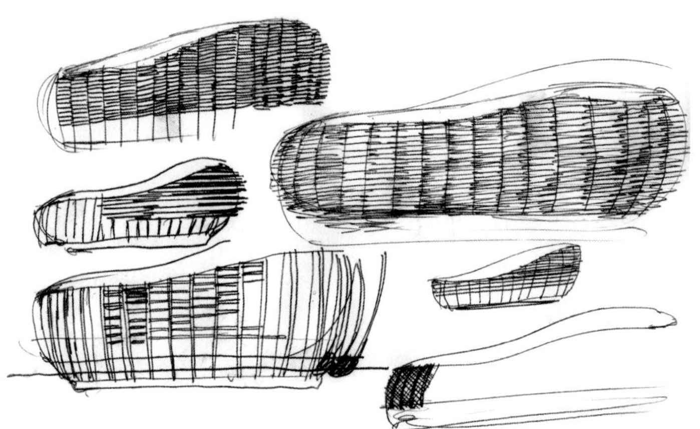

Preparatory sketch by Michele De Lucchi

The UniCredit Pavilion; in the background, the Porta Nuova UniCredit tower

UniCredit

The UniCredit Pavilion blends well with the urban context and green landscaping of the area

View of construction site

Section view of the pavilion

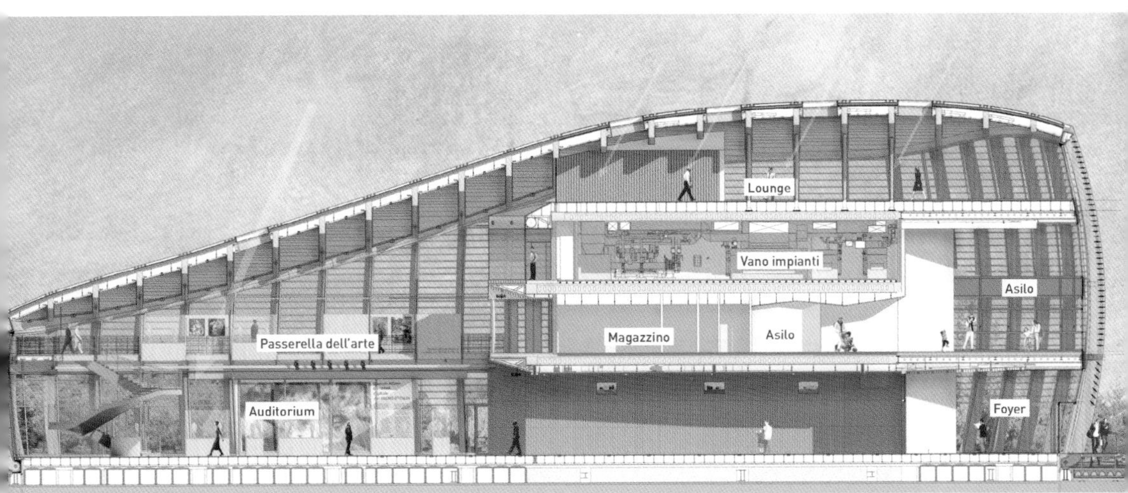
Lounge
Vano impianti
Asilo
Passerella dell'arte
Magazzino
Asilo
Auditorium
Foyer

13 **E3_East Office Building**
Porta Nuova

MCA Mario Cucinella Architects

The proposed project for the E3-East office building completes the Porta Nuova Varesine complex performing a dual role: it acts as an entrance gate, linking the urban fabric to the adjacent green park, and also as a design concept strongly representative of the business and administration theme of the area.

The building is conceived as a scenographic backdrop and explores the synthesis between the "natural" and the "artificial" from both a formal and environmental perspective.

The E3 project by MCA Mario Cucinella Architects is located in an extremely vibrant architectural context only a short distance from Piazza Gae Aulenti. The ratio between the scale of the intervention and the pre-existing constructions inspired the search for a project solution with strong aesthetic and dimensional unity.

The new project is designed as a volume enclosed between two sheets of wooden centring that form a kind of "tree bark"; the structural and visual lightness allows the building to blend effortlessly in a context where the existing architectural structures have strong impact and are charged with symbolism. This building is not conceived as a new "personality" but as a flexible space, configured for office and commercial use, placing the emphasis on the relation between interior and exterior.

Sobriety, rhythm, and restraint are the characteristics that have made the great Milanese architectural school so widely acclaimed.
A.M.

Side elevation

Rendered project

General layout

Photo of model

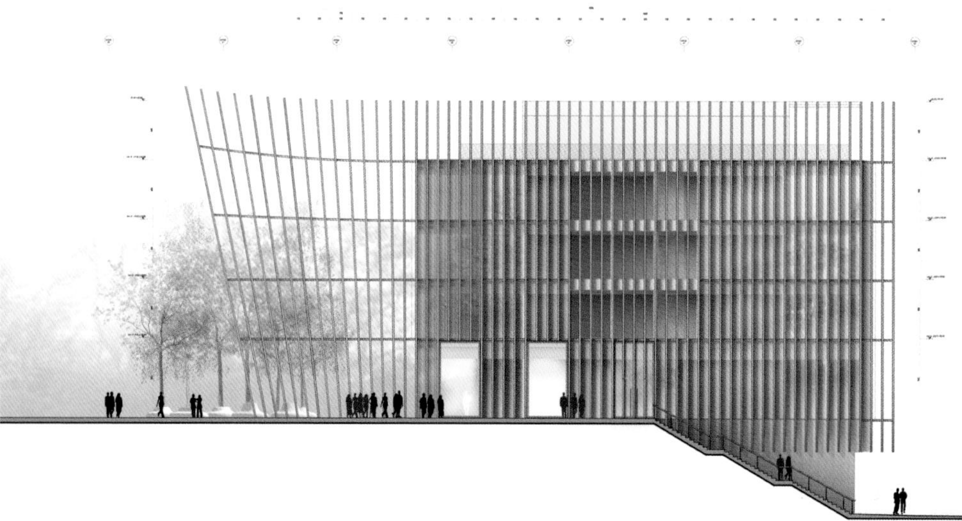

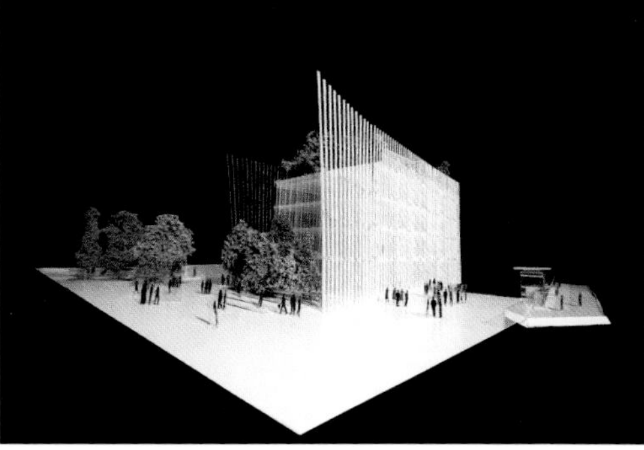

14 Porta Nuova Varesine

Arquitectonica, Caputo Partnership,
Antonio Citterio Patricia Viel and Partners,
Coima Image, Dolce Vita Homes,
Kohn Pedersen Fox Associates, LAND,
Studio M2P Associati

Porta Nuova Varesine links up with Porta Nuova Garibaldi through the elevated walkway over Via Melchiorre Gioia — forming the longest pedestrian circuit in the city, with more than 900 metres of paths and walkways. This district is composed of a range of very different elements including residential buildings, office space, shopping malls and public areas.

Overlooking Via Melchiorre Gioia, the complex rises in a strategic position in relation to the Porta Nuova district, defining a central public square called Piazza Alvar Aalto; it is composed of three residential towers: Aria and Solaria, designed by Arquitectonica of Miami, and Solea, developed by the Milanese firm, Caputo Partnership.

The towers are raised above the street level thanks to a podium system. Solaria has 34 floors and Aria, 17 floors, to which another floor has been added, destined for residents' services and the two main entrances located on two levels; both buildings blend harmoniously in the landscape with its high-rise skyline. The two buildings designed by Arquitectonica have a similar layout. From the front, they seem identical; each floor has large double-height windows and wide terrace-balconies with frosted and transparent glass parapets planted with lush green terrace gardens. The interiors were designed and furnished by Dolce Vita Homes in collaboration with Antonio Citterio Patricia Viel and Partners and Coima Image.

Solea, designed by Caputo Partnership, is a fifteen-storey building; apart from the two main entrances set on two levels, it reveals a more complex style of architecture, characterised by the deconstruction of certain volumes. The tower appears like a white crystal, open at the corners with views from the loggias that overlook the city.

All three buildings were awarded LEED GOLD certification thanks to close attention focussed on environmental sustainability, constructive systems and materials employed.

Located east of the three residential towers is the Porta Nuova Varesine Business District. Created from the vision of the American firm, Kohn Pedersen Fox Associates (KPF), this complex is composed of three buildings with strict elegant lines: two lower buildings and a third taller building close the complex. This tower presents the most innovative solution in the project and is destined for offices; it rises 130 metres into the Milan skyline and has been called the Diamond Tower because of its irregular prismatic transparent form. Careful project design and choice of materials and technologies won the building LEED GOLD certification, one of the highest recognitions awarded by the Green Building Council to eco-sustainable buildings.

Opposite the Kohn Pedersen Fox Associates building are the Ville di Porta Nuova (residential homes), designed by Studio M2P Associati. These new constructions are inspired by traditional residential home models and were also awarded LEED GOLD certification.

Studio Land designed the green landscaping that connects the two main piazzas with a wide walkway: Porta Est is linked with Piazza Lina Bo Bardi, based on the project by Antonio Citterio Patricia Viel and Partners, and with Piazza Alvar Aalto. The green spaces surround the promenade, a continuous pedestrian walkway that links up the individual architectural interventions with the surrounding urban spaces for easier transit. The green areas are furnished with seating and decorative elements that recall the atmosphere of the Biblioteca degli alberi in Porta Nuova Isola.

A.M.

View of the elevated walkway connecting Piazza Gae Aulenti and Porta Nuova Varesine

On the left, the three buildings of the Porta Nuova Business District Varesine, a project by Kohn Pedersen Fox Associates (KPF); on the right, Le Ville di Porta Nuova, designed by Studio M2P Associati. Studio Land was responsible for the green landscaping design

The Aria and Solaria buildings on the right, designed by Arquitectonica, create a dialogue with the KPF towers

The facetted volume of the Solea tower, developed by the Milanese company, Caputo Partnership

The spaces under Piazza Lina Bo Bardi were designed by Antonio Citterio, Patricia Viel and Partners

UniCredit

15 **Gioiaotto**

Via Melchiorre Gioia

Park Associati

The project by the Milanese firm, Park Associati, approached this modern architecture restoration by studying the project by Marco Zanuso and Pietro Crescini completed in 1973. Originally called Residence Porta Nuova, the project is an important landmark of the architecture of the period, typical of a certain Milanese spirit at the time.

Park Associati was the winner of a competition by invitation organised in 2012 by Hines Italia, who own the building in question. The project involves restyling the facades, revisitation of the ground floor, and restructuring the internal spaces that will be divided into hotel and office spaces.

The "horizontal" matrix, one of the building's main features, has been maintained. The project focussed on the connection at street level as one of the strong points, to underline the contrast with the verticality of the new skyscrapers of Porta Nuova.

The analysis of Zanuso's work was a delicate subject that implied in-depth study of the building; the intervention required a level of architectural sensitivity that could ensure that the historical memory was maintained, and at the same time, offer the required internal flexibility and luminosity in line with contemporary architecture.

The project plan focussed immediately on detail as one of the main elements. In the entry hall coarse surfaces refracting the light contrast with the reflective surfaces.

On the exterior, the project paid great attention to the window openings, the only element of the facade that was transformed, giving the building a totally new expression. Inside, large strip windows divided vertically in three, follow the horizontal structure of the building. The window opening is underlined by glass fins that increase the internal flexibility allowing the free installation of possible future mobile wall partitions.

On the other hand, in the hotel side, the existing window openings are emphasised by alternating transparent glass sheets, arranged in an irregular pattern divided by fins and wooden frames.

On the ground floor, the facade alternates transparent modules and opaque structural elements covered by screen-printed windows on two levels to increase the three dimensional effect of the facade.

The building was awarded LEED Platinum certification for energy efficiency and ecological impact.
A.M.

View of the entrance

The top floor features an elegant glassed-in superelevated structure

The "horizontal" matrix, one of the outstanding features of the project, is clearly visible on the facades

Facade detail

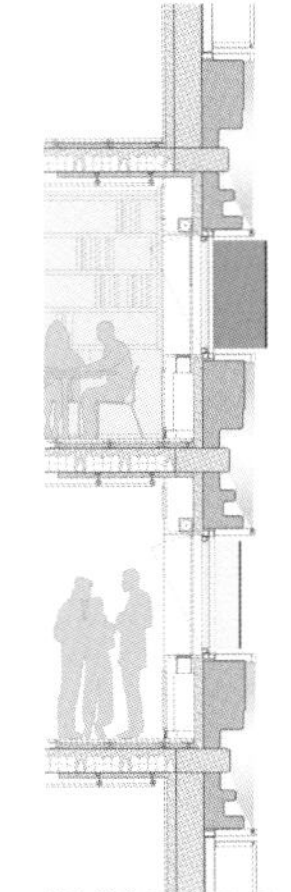

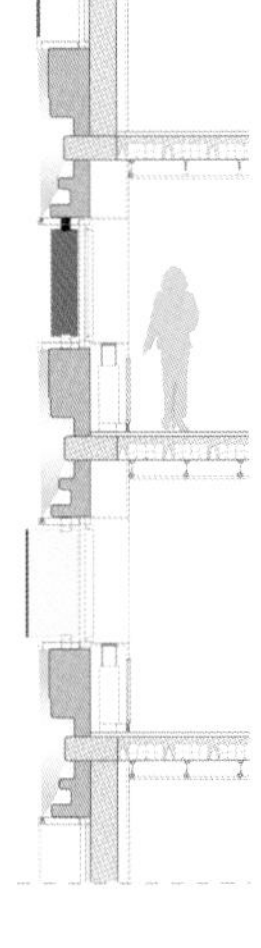

16 Porta Nuova Isola

Boeri Studio, Inside Outside,
William McDonough + Partners,
Lucien Lagrange Architects,
Baukuh Architetti

The Porta Nuova Isola project completes the Masterplan intervention towards the north and includes several extremely refined architectural constructions.

The Bosco verticale complex designed by Boeri Studio is the new landmark in the area, towering over the Giardino De Castillia. The project is composed of two separate buildings: two towers, 110 and 76 metres in height, featuring terraces and balconies planted with 480 medium to large sized plants, 250 small trees, 14,000 climbing plants, and 5000 shrubs, the equivalent of 2,5 acres of forest. The Bosco Verticale (Vertical woods) was the prizewinner of the international Highrise Award for 2014. As well as introducing a new concept of symbiosis between architecture and nature, it increases plant and animal biodiversity, helping to enrich Milan with a model of habitation innovation and quality.

The large park, La Biblioteca degli alberi, connects the Giardino De Castillia to the Gae Aulenti piazza and to the adjacent urban areas of Porta Nuova, the pedestrian circuits of the Garibaldi area, and to the Melchiorre Gioia overhead walkway. Within the park, designed and landscaped by Inside Outside, is a mosaic of different itineraries enriched with themed gardens, lawns and trees, and aromatic herb and flower gardens. In Via Gaetano De Castillia is the Fondazione Riccardo Catella, an example of industrial architecture returned to the city as a social space dedicated to culture, design, civic initiatives and refreshment area; close by is the Incubatore per l'arte, designed by Boeri Studio, one of the new public buildings for the city of Milan, established to preserve and encourage the social and cultural activities of the Stecca degli Artigiani. The new rectangular building rises on the site of the former industrial building; the exterior features clean plain lines clad in metal panelling, while the interior has been designed to cater to a range of different activities with extremely neutral and flexible spaces. It resembles a type of covered gallery connecting the city with the new park.

The Porta Nuova Isola area is completed with the Business District Isola designed by William McDonough + Partners, previously the headquarters of Google Italia and Pandora; it also includes the apartment buildings, Residenze dei Giardini designed by Lucien Lagrange Architects, and la Casa della memoria museum by Studio Associato Baukuh, a sober rectangular building with its "narrative" facade that collects, preserves and narrates the historical memory of Milan through personal stories and actual testimonies.

Although not part of the original Masterplan envisaged by Pelli and the Hines group, a short distance away will be the new Civic Centre of the Isola-Garibaldi quarter. The project competition was won by the young architects of studio KM 429 architettura. The civic centre is designed to recall the history of Milan, with a clean streamlined building that embraces the diversified urban landscape while focussing on its integration with the park and the neighbourhood, presenting an image of solid simplicity.

A.M.

opposite page
The "Incubatore per l'Arte" that houses spaces destined for artisanal activities and cultural associations is a rectangular construction on two levels, with a total surface of 800 square metres

Bosco Verticale, designed by Boeri Studio, is composed of two towers featuring balconies planted with hundreds of trees and shrubs

The new Centro Civico in the Isola-Garibaldi area, winning project by studio KM 429 architettura

General view of the Porta Nuova, Garibaldi and Isola area

UniCredit

17 **V33**

Residential apartment building

Via Volturno

Vudafieri Saverino Partners

The original building was constructed in 1964 and was the former Communist Party headquarters in Milan. The facade was clad in red glass and aluminium, and the building was located on the outskirts of the city. Today the V33 building has become a landmark and an important connecting link between the new urban district under construction in Porta Nuova and the older traditional Isola neighbourhood. The restructuration involves transforming the pre-existing tower, raising it with the addition of seven new floors to create a dialogue with the new skyscrapers in the Porta Nuova district.

On the facades, the use of concrete, black clinker, and glossy anodised aluminium, popular elements in Milanese architecture in the 1950s and 1960s, express a dialectical choice between tradition and modernity.

The strict severity of the facade is softened by the addition of bow windows in open work aluminium sheeting, virtual volumes filled with climbing plants, forming architectural filters between the interior and the urban landscape.

Part of an existing urban block, the main entrance to the tower is in Via Volturno that gives access to the apartment building and the first level of the underground garage. The ground floor has a shopping centre, lobby-reception and bicycle storage room. On the mezzanine floor, there is planted terrace and the condominium fitness gym.

The fourteen-floor building houses about twenty apartments of different sizes: the areas have been mainly designed as loft space, with spacious living areas open to the exterior through glass walls and large covered terraces. The west side is composed of loggia balconies, while on the east side the bow windows are protected by special gold metal openwork screens.

The project has used sustainable materials with low environmental impact focussed on eco-compatibility.

The intervention has paid close attention to heat and acoustic insulation: the external porous brick walls have external insulation to eliminate thermal bridges caused by wall deformity. The internal multilayer and multi-material double walls provide excellent acoustic insulation.

The top floor is destined to house systems installations and equipment, flue and emission pipes, as well as the solar panels that integrate the hot water production for the heating system, making a considerable contribution to the building s energy efficiency.

A.M.

Detail of the bow window screened by openwork aluminium sheeting

Front view from Via Volturno

M

18 **Istituto Gonzaga**
Via Vitruvio / Via Settembrini

One Works

The Gonzaga College of Milan has a long history of continuous transformations that have made the school a pioneer since the beginning of the twentieth century for the focus placed on extracurricular, sports and recreational activities.

This important educational complex is home to famous works of art, la Pietà by Lucio Fontana (1957) and the bas-relief, Da cento anni educhiamo al futuro by Benedetto Pietrogrande (2007) and dedicates a great deal of space to student activities, enriched by the recent transformations that have provided a new sports centre with swimming pool and gym, an auditorium, and a wide range of service areas that are also open to the local community.

The concept of new multifunctional complex is based on three principles:

- educational: Gonzaga College offers its students excellent services;

- urbanistic: the project uses urban densification as an instrument to increase services for the city;

- economical: the school sold land under the property that has been used to build an underground car park, thus creating the funding to carry out the other interventions.

The project is composed of three buildings that enclose an internal, tree-planted courtyard, one of the main hubs of student activities. The lowest structure with self-supporting metal cladding houses the access ramp to the underground parking; the glassed building overlooking the courtyard contains the complex distribution system leading to all departments; the translucid building houses the sports facilities, swimming pool and large gym, and can be used by the local population who can access the facilities through the new entrance in Via Settembrini. The auditorium was built in the pre-existing lower building, taking advantage of the space previously occupied by the former gym. The intervention is characterised by an interesting financial-management program that permits self-financing of the project, ensuring the continuation of the educational program without interruption, and restoring the courtyard for student use in the shortest possible time.
A.M.

Longitudinal section

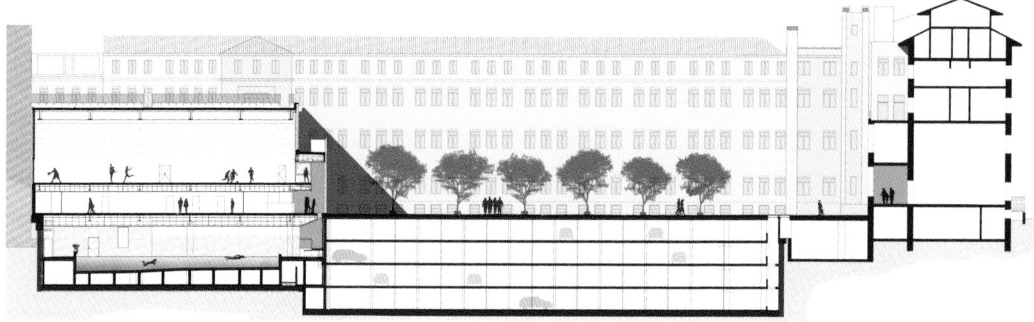

Nocturnal view of the complex

The facade of the building that houses the sports gym

19 City Pavilion
Piazza Duca d'Aosta

Vudafieri Saverino Partners

The City Pavilion was designed by the Milanese architectural firm, Vudafieri Saverino Partners. It is a Chinese-Italian project aimed at developing collaboration between Shanghai and Milan, a venture strongly promoted by the two cities to celebrate the 45th anniversary of the opening of diplomatic relations between China and Italy.

City Pavilion is located in one of the nerve centres in Milan in Piazza Duca d'Aosta, opposite the main Milan railway station and the Pirelli Tower. It is the only pavilion in the city centre, designed as a support for the three Chinese pavilions within the Expo 2015 grounds. Positioned in a strategic location for visibility and easy access, the building is a home for both cultures, a showcase for Italian and Chinese products of excellence and a base in the city to present Expo 2015, for exchange and contacts.

Tiziano Vudafieri and Claudio Saverino were responsible for both the architectural project and the interior design. With consolidated professional experience in both cities, they were able to interpret the essence of both countries with a synthesis drawn from the best traditions of Italian design. The architects commented: "The dynamic geometry of a heron's wing was the basic composition structure for this architectural design. Lightness, order and balance among all the elements. A free open layout, pure glass volume, space outdoors inspired by the atrium of the domus italica, surrounded by a portico with graphic design of powerful impact. It symbolises the exact image of the pavilion concept".

The space is transparent and light with strong graphical impact, built from white metal, dark and light coloured woods and glass. It is a travelling structure that can be easily integrated in an urban context, combining the Italian concept of the portico and the Chinese pagoda-shaped roof.

The glassed area is divided into three distinct zones: the showroom, the official reception area and the food & beverage area, and covers a total surface of 360 square metres. The internal exhibition space hosts fashion and design companies as well as events showcasing art and culture of excellence.

Following the Expo fair in Milan, the City Pavilion will be disassembled, ready for reassembly in other locations. A travelling pavilion, ready to be recycled and reused in line with contemporary principles of eco-sustainability.

A.M.

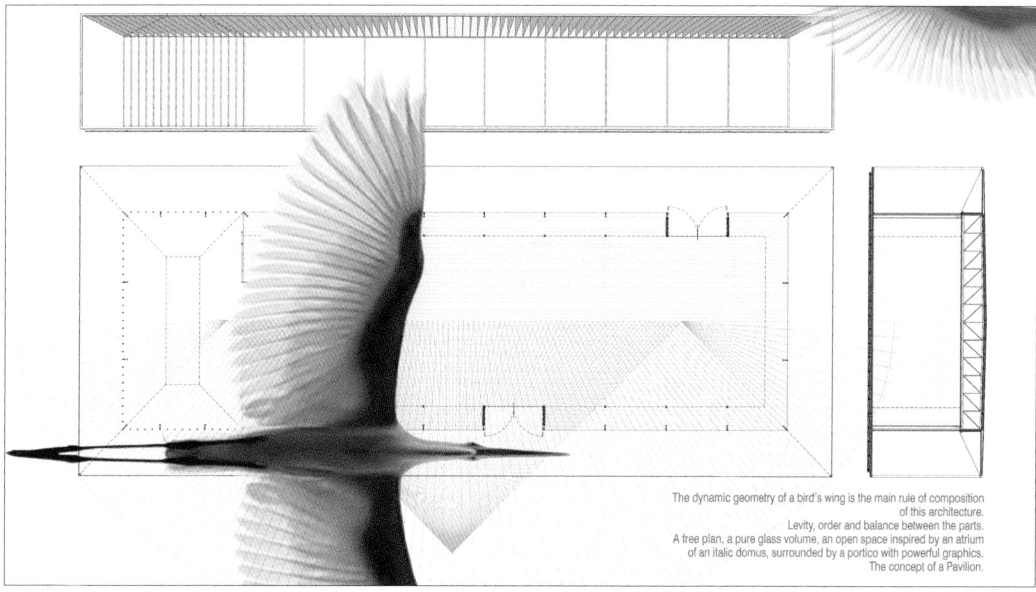

City Pavilion in its temporary location in Piazza Duca d'Aosta, opposite the Milan Central Station

Views by day and by night

Constructive concept of the City Pavilion

Outskirts of Milan

20. Museo delle Culture - MUDEC
Via Tortona

21. CityLife
Piazzale Giulio Cesare

22. Allianz Tower
CityLife

23. Piazza Tre Torri
CityLife

24. Conversion of the Portello Area
Viale Scarampo

25. IULM University of Language and Communication Knowledge Transfer Center, KTC
Via Carlo Bo

26. Headquarters of the Fondazione Prada
Largo Isarco

27. Carlo Erba Apartment building
Piazza Carlo Erba

28. Residential Apartment Building
Via Tiraboschi

29. Residenze Montegani
Via Montegani

30. La Forgiatura
Via Varesina

20 **Museo delle Culture - MUDEC**

Via Tortona

This urban museum is located within the decommissioned industrial complex on the site of the former Ansaldo plant in Milan. With geometrical, but differently shaped structures and facades that conceal intricate internal spaces, this project was aimed at emphasising the inevitably hidden qualities of the existing site. In fact, the Ansaldo complex is a collection of industrial buildings that required restoration and redesigning to recover new spaces.

The new Ansaldo project is destined for public and private services. Alongside the existing buildings, the project incorporates a new structure that replaces several buildings that had to be demolished. The spaces in the first floor exhibition area, located around a large sinuous covered piazza, house the permanent collection and rooms dedicated to important temporary exhibitions. The complex also includes services for the public such as a bistro, design store, Cultural Forum space, multifunctional area, lecture room, an art restoration workshop, and an area dedicated to children's activities.

The new museum is composed of a series of cubic configurations clad in titanium-zinc panels with a central illuminated glass structure. The organic geometry with its unusual "flower" form is in strong contrast with the other buildings. An intervention where the traditional internal-external concept is reversed through clever manipulation plus the necessary dovetailing and communication between the various cubes that recall the industrial structures located inside the complex and neighbouring sites. Consequently, the intermediate spaces become part of a formal sequence of external courtyards and passageways, creating an interwoven blend of old and new architectures within a new cultural centre, important for Milan.

G.P.

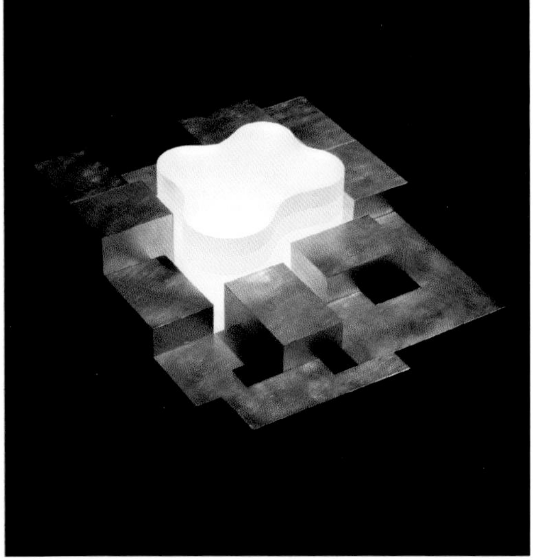

Model of the building

Building seen from the exterior

External shell

following pages
The internal piazza covered by an organic geometrical glass structure

21 **CityLife**
Piazzale Giulio Cesare

Zaha Hadid LTD, Arata Isozaki & Associates, Studio Daniel Libeskind

Following the transfer of much of the exhibition to the new Rho-Pero centre, the new liberated area of approximately 366,000 square meters, comes the new Milan CityLife district designed by Zaha Hadid, Arata Isozaki, and Daniel Libeskind.

The project involves a detailed and balanced mix of public and private facilities and areas, including residences, offices, a park and green areas, services, culture, shopping and leisure.

Following an international competition, the project for the large public nature park, which will provide an ecological link between the north-west green area and the Sempione Park of approximately 170,000 square meters, was assigned to the Gustafson Porter studio (UK), working as a group with !Melk and One Works.

The focus of CityLife is the large central square, which will be served by the new Tre Torri station for the MM5 subway, and will in fact overlook the three towers in the CityLife Business District. Designed by Zaha Hadid, Arata Isozaki and Daniel Libeskind, the three towers, which will be characterized by their highly iconic nature, enriching the entire city skyline, represent a strong symbol of the city's transformation.

There are plans to create a Shopping District at the foot of the towers, with a rich and diverse range of restaurants, bars, shops and services. To the south of the business district, however, are the residences designed by Zaha Hadid and Daniel Libeskind.

The residential lot, designed by Zaha Hadid, composed of seven buildings of heights varying from five to thirteen floors, is located southeast of CityLife and faces the park on one side, along Via Senofonte - Piazza Giulio Cesare. The outline of the rooftops has a continuous and sinuous movement that becomes a key design element in the entire complex. The curved lines of the balconies define the facade's movement which in turn echoes the landscape below.

The residences designed by Daniel Libeskind, divided into eight buildings of heights ranging again from five to thirteen floors, are located on the southwest side of the area and overlook the park on one side, along Via Spinola - Piazza Giulio Cesare. The project originated from the volumetric study of a court plan, segmented and recomposed to create open scheme structures that work in relation to each other and the environment. The layout of the buildings on the lots is designed to guarantee a permeable system with green corridors and optical cones that connect the park to the existing neighbourhoods.

M.G.M.

Libeskind apartment buildings overlooking the park

View of the Hadid residential buildings from Via Senofonte

following pages
Overall view of the intervention

22 **Allianz Tower**
CityLife

Arata Isozaki with Andrea Maffei Architects

The Allianz Tower, designed by Arata Isozaki with Andrea Maffei Architects, with its 202 metres of height (207 considering the city plan), is the tallest building in the CityLife area.

To be used as offices, it covers 50 floors and 50,000 square meters, accommodating up to 3,800 people.

The architectural concept, inspired by Brancusi's model of the endless column, becomes a construction metaphor without limitations, aspiring to the maximum verticality expressed through the creation of modular façade systems replicated throughout its height. In fact, as pointed out by the architect Andrea Maffei, "With Isozaki we thought of an endless skyscraper, made up of six-storey modules characterized by a curved facade that could ideally continue into infinity."[1]

"When I was asked to present a design project to redevelop the Trade Fair area", said architect Arata Isozaki, "I thought about what the future of Milan would be like. The first time I came here there were still a few quite tall buildings, the Torre Velasca and the Pirellone. Both have a very important symbolic meaning, and we haven't ignored that. In the study for the design we thought about the symbolic meaning that the skyscraper would have. So we tried to create something unique, also taking care over the liveability and environmental sustainability."

The building rests on a foundation slab of 5,300 cubic metres of reinforced concrete, under which 62 poles were sunk 31 metres deep. It is characterized by a structure with cores of reinforced concrete, mixed pillars with steel cores, and "girders" positioned at the twenty-fourth floor and on the rooftop to bind together the main cores. At the foot of the tower, four struts of a gold colour, 40 to 60 metres in height, composed of elements in steel and forgings, expertly combine design and engineering, in other words, an aesthetic element with a structural function.

The glass facade, highly transparent, covers an area of 24,000 square meters and consists of about 4,500 "cell" elements.

On the short sides of the tower run fourteen lifts, including three completely transparent ones on each side to offer a panoramic view of the city.

As for the internal distribution, the building is characterized by an extremely flexible modulation of the environments. Moreover, thanks to the floor-to-ceiling windows, work spaces are completely illuminated with natural light.

The tower is well-connected to the urban fabric through a system of underground roads that provides vehicular access to parking, in addition to direct connection with the underground. In fact, passing through the commercial area, it is possible to reach the office spaces from the station of the new M5 line in the heart of the Piazza Tre Torri in the CityLife area.

The building is designed for maximum efficiency and to reduce energy costs; it will be powered mainly by renewable energy sources, including district heating and photovoltaic panels. Thanks to the special attention given to this, it has already received LEED pre-certification, qualifying it as level GOLD.

M.G.M.

[1]Arata Isozaki in Milan: visiting the CityLife tower with his design architect, Milan, 29 October.

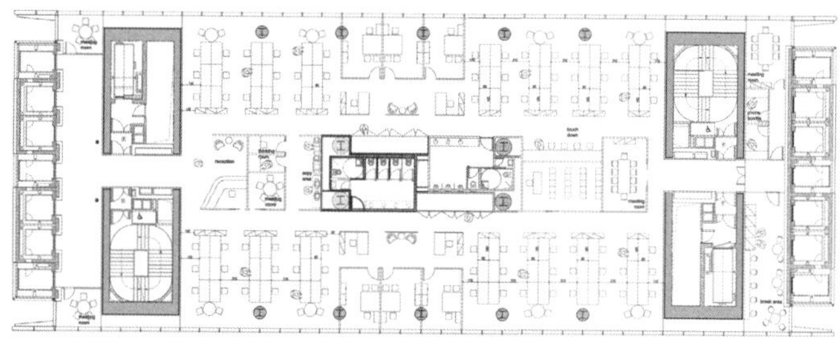

Typical floor plan
with potential layout

Views of Allianz Tower
silhouetted against
the CityLife area

23 **Piazza Tre Torri**
CityLife

One Works

CityLife is a vast redevelopment project in the heart of Milan where Fieramilanocity began operating back in 2005. After participating in the international competition in 2010 for the 168,000 square metre urban park project, One Works was awarded first prize and assigned the Piazza Tre Torri project with a team under the direction of Gustafson Porter. The project also includes the adjacent commercial area located on the lower level.

The project for the piazza was born from the desire to construct a single space that would strongly connect the different levels of the area located between the three Isozaki, Hadid and Libeskind towers. The main entrance to the towers is located +129 metres a.s.l., while the sunken piazza level is at +122 metres a.s.l. The configuration of the piazza is aimed at emphasising three different aspects: the route between the northern and southern parts of the park; the route between east and west that connects Piazza Sei Febbraio with the fashion mall situated in the lower floor of the Hadid tower and the west park; and lastly, the central aspect, making Piazza Tre Torri the meeting point of the two circuits.

Set over the grid of horizontal link-ups, are the vertical links connecting the two access levels to the towers that form the two public reference heights for the whole project, with the subway station and underground parking.

The large size of the piazza determined the choice for projecting roofs to create a human scale in a space prevalently dominated by the skyline of the towers, in a dialogue with the whole urban landscape.

Green spaces are designed inside the piazza to highlight the different natures of the various areas. The largest portion is located on the eastern side to create continuity between north and south, and another is placed opposite the entrance to the fashion mall to create greater intimity for the outdoor space of the restaurants that overlook the piazza. Groups of trees will be planted in the paved areas to accentuate the route towards the Palazzo dei Congressi. The two larger openings are surrounded by planted flower borders.
M.G.M.

General layout of the piazza

Rendered project

View of the piazza; pool in the foreground

24 **Conversion of the Portello Area**
Viale Scarampo

Studio Valle Architetti Associati, Cino Zucchi Architetti / Zucchi & Partners, Canali Associati, Charles Jencks, Andreas Kipar – LAND, Topotek 1, Arup

The Portello conversion project, developed by Studio Valle and completed in 2011, was constructed on the site previously occupied by the Alfa Romeo plants. The project was aimed at reconstructing the urban fabric in a zone dominated by the presence of a huge infrastructural system that had fallen in disuse and had remained disconnected from the city centre. Portello is located along the Sempione-San Siro axis on the edge of the motorway system and shielded by the Milan Fair Pavilions designed by Mario Bellini.

The Studio Valle master plan provided for a series of large-scale architectural interventions in proportion with the massive infrastructures in the area but without relinquishing the urban character of the intervention. This character was obtained through the intelligent integration of walking and cycling paths, piazzas, porticos, and loggias that the designers have incorporated to maintain a sense of continuity with the historic centre.

The three office buildings are located in the fan-shaped piazza, the largest in Milan, called Piazza Gino Valle, dedicated to the "historical" father of the project, realised in collaboration with the Berlin firm, Topotek 1. The piazza is enriched with a bas-relief by Emilio Isgrò: Grande Cancellatura per Giovanni Testori.

The bridge that crosses Viale Serra was designed by ARUP Associati, while the large urban park — designed by the American architect and theorist Charles Jencks and created with Andreas Kipar - LAND — includes a series of walking and cycling paths that serve the residential zones, designed respectively by C. Zucchi and G. Canali, and that lead to the shopping mall (Studio Valle), where a sail-like overhead shelter closes the route at Piazzale Accursio.

The large 70,000-square metre urban park marks the access to the metropolitan subway line arriving from Milan (from Malpensa airport or the Rho Fairgrounds). The ground has been modelled to create a sculptural effect to maintain continuity with the existing area represented by Monte Stella, the iconic artificial hill created with bomb rubble after the war by Piero Bottoni. The matrix of this project is based on the desire to establish links with places and periods of the city and its territory; it is expressed visually in the geometry of the circles, arcs and crescents, echoed in the shapes and finishes of the paving. In an even greater relationship with the city, the Portello Park is also part of a green circuit of walking and cycling paths: the so-called "raggi verdi" conceived by Andreas Kipar - LAND, cross over the tangenziale ring roads to connect the centre of Milan with the hinterland.
R.M.

View of Piazza Gino Valle, overlooked by three buildings designed by the same architect in collaboration with Topotek 1

Apartment buildings designed by Cino Zucchi Architetti

Aerial view; in the foreground, apartment buildings by Canali Associati

following pages
Aerial view; on the left, urban park designed by Charles Jencks and Andreas Kipar, Land — the Milan Fairground urban centre buildings can be seen on the right

25 **IULM University of Language and Communication Knowledge Transfer Center, KTC**
Via Carlo Bo

5+1AA

The project for the expansion of IULM (University of Language and Communication of Milan), also known as the Knowledge Transfer Center, aims at creating a space where the city can enter the university and the university can open up its knowledge to the city.

Located in the consolidated suburb of Barona, the building will complete the existing university campus complex, and will be developed as an urban system, where the perimeter will be permanently open to the complex aspects of the city around it. There are no boundaries between the courtyard of the new intervention and the urban fabric; walkways and green areas are continuously interspersed among the solid blocks of the buildings, offering parallel and alternative itineraries.

A simple rectangular footprint coordinates the refined balance between the solids and voids of the whole complex, creating a structure composed of three main elements designed to have functions that are independent, but complementary with each other. The red brick and glass tower, symbol and heart of the new specialised spaces of the university, marks the beginning of a route completely directed towards the future. The interior rotates around a helical staircase, and as well as the archives and reference rooms, the building will also house the digital library, one of the key strengths of the IULM university project. This will provide the possibility of viewing, recording, and processing vast amounts of material relating to communications. The southern building, with its low linear profile, will incorporate flexible and usable spaces for the academic structure — lecture rooms, laboratories, offices, as well as for potential space for journalistic, television and industrial communications companies. The auditorium will represent another essential element of the complex: the audacious size of the auditorium is well suited to the ambitions of the university that aspires to an international reputation and to the prestigious events it organises.

The project seems to create a camouflage effect with the surrounding context in the choice of materials: red brick, exposed concrete, glass and plaster finish. It is the story of the city through the colours and reflections of its multiple facets.
V.M.

Longitudinal section
of the complex

External elevation of the
Knowledge Transfer Center

The red brick and glass tower,
symbol and heart of the
new specialised spaces
of the university

Low linear building on
southern side

26 **Headquarters of the Fondazione Prada**
Largo Isarco

OMA/Rem Koolhaas

Since its establishment, the Prada Foundation, created in 1993 by Miuccia Prada and Patrizio Bertelli, has been an institution dedicated to art and culture. The new Milanese headquarters, which opened in 2015, were built after a design by the architectural firm OMA, led by Rem Koolhaas, and explore the different artistic languages through a vast repertoire of spatial types. Located on Largo Isarco, in the south of Milan, the complex extends over a total area of 19,000 square metres, of which 11,000 will be used for exhibitions. The work explores the relationship between art, contemporary architecture and the theme of recovering a historically significant industrial area. The words of the designer perfectly summarize the character of the project which "is neither a work of conservation nor the creation of a new architecture. These two dimensions coexist, while remaining distinct. Old and new, horizontal and vertical, wide and narrow, black and white, open and closed: these contrasts determine the variety of challenges that describe the concept behind the new Fondazione."

The complex — a large courtyard with early twentieth-century buildings within it — had an unusual variety of spaces, some with a very pronounced industrial character, others more residential. Visiting the Fondazione, one moves between environments that have very different spatial characteristics and intended uses. The first building you will see as you enter from Largo Isarco is the Podium: a cube with three transparent fronts surmounted by a beam-shaped parallelepiped. The Podium is the cornerstone building, ideally connecting the other architectural episodes. The Haunted House, on the other hand, will be used for installations. The golden colour of its walls centralizes its position within the spatial configuration.

The central area of the complex houses a cinema with a roof garden.

A tower of nine levels hosts a series of galleries for installations, each with different spatial qualities, equipped to meet different exhibition needs.

The southern and northern oblong structures are home to a series of galleries. The southern structure, moreover, is the access area to the Deposito, the most extensive exhibition area in the complex.

The building at the entrance of the new centre will welcome the public with two spaces designed through special collaborations: an educational area developed with the students of the École nationale supérieure d'architecture de Versailles and a bar, conceived by director Wes Anderson, recreating the atmosphere of typical Milanese cafés.

At the opening of the new Milan headquarters, Fondazione Prada will host a number of activities. The works of the Prada collection will be presented in thematic exhibitions, Robert Gober and Thomas Demand will create site-specific installations to interact with the industrial architecture and new spaces, and Roman Polanski will explore the suggestions that have inspired his films.

A.M./R.M.

View of the new Prada Foundation headquarters in Milan: architectural project by OMA
Photo: Bas Princen 2015, courtesy of the Prada Foundation

Rendering of the intervention on the ex-distillery

Details of the new Prada Foundation headquarters in Milan: architectural project by OMA
Photo: Bas Princen 2015, courtesy of the Prada Foundation

View of the cafeteria, designed by Wes Anderson

27 **Carlo Erba Apartment building**
Piazza Carlo Erba

Eisenman Architects, Degli Esposti Architetti, AZ Studio

Continuous facades, urban blocks, density and window views were the main characteristics of Milanese medium-sized residential buildings chosen by the architects as a focus to recapture a style that was popular following the Second World War.

The triangular shape of the city block led the team (Eisenman, Degli Esposti, and Zuliani) to abandon the idea of a continuous facade since any type of internal courtyard would have reduced interior lighting. They decided on a single sinuous line construction in an incomplete S shape able to provide good quality external open spaces. A large condominium garden composed of green terraced levels slopes down from the Via Pinturicchio perimeter towards the various entrances to the building.

The building is composed of a layer system that underlines the variations in the facades. The three lower floors, clad in travertine stone, form the base of the building while the second layer is composed of the fourth floor, slightly recessed from the facade and faced with Carrara marble. The fifth and sixth floors with light coloured cladding are enclosed in a white metal grid structure that frames both floors and emphasises the horizontal line of the building. This white framework encloses the construction and provides a uniform height for the top three floors that are composed of ìurban residencesî. These elements project out from the main volume of the building and echo the tiered structure of the seventh, eighth and ninth floors.

Refined, quality travertine and marble materials have been used on the external facades and the internal floors and walls are finished with natural wood and stone. The spacious luminous entrances and common areas are double-height volumes with a play of lowered ceiling areas and profile lighting that define the waiting areas for guests, information area and connecting areas to other levels of the building. The apartments have been designed with a wide range of unique solutions and great attention has been paid to the sunlight orientation in the various internal spaces.
C.G.

Intervention layout

Rendered project, view from Via Giovanni Pascoli

Rendered project

28 **Residential Apartment Building**
Via Tiraboschi

BerettaAssociati

This intervention is located next to Piazzale Libia at the intersection between Via Tiraboschi, Via Muratori and Via Lattuada, and is set in a residential area featuring large neighbourhood blocks and a wide range of architectural styles from the early nineteenth century to the present day.

The new construction will be located on a plot that was previously occupied by a building that has been demolished, and the project aims to entirely cover the incumbent blank facade of the adjacent nine-storey building. To achieve this, the building has been aligned with the eaves of the adjacent construction and will be developed in a mainly vertical style. The living space is arranged so that each floor contains a single apartment.

The layout of each apartment has been carefully designed, placing the bedrooms on the side of the internal garden, while the living rooms overlook the street through deep loggia terraces equipped with planters and motorised sunshade systems that help increase the building's energy performance.

The basements can accommodate 21 garages accessed from the street using a car elevator system.

Pietra di Grolla stone is used for the external facades while the window frames have been built with aluminium thermal break profiles.

The internal systems in the building have been studied carefully to guarantee maximum energy saving, achieving Class A category certification thanks to energy produced by an gas heating pump vista integrated with solar power. The air exchange is obtained through an independent heat regenerator.
M.G.M.

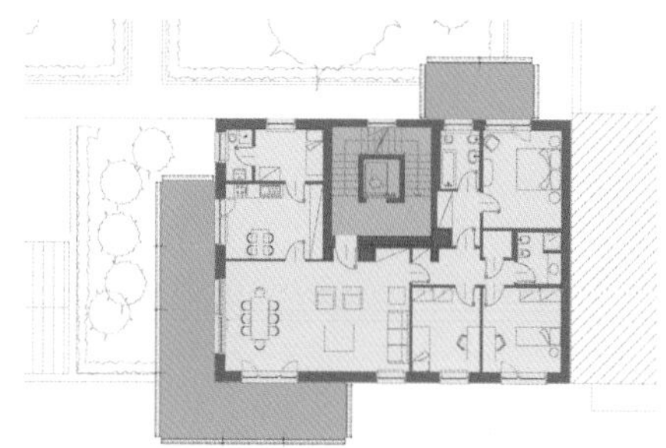

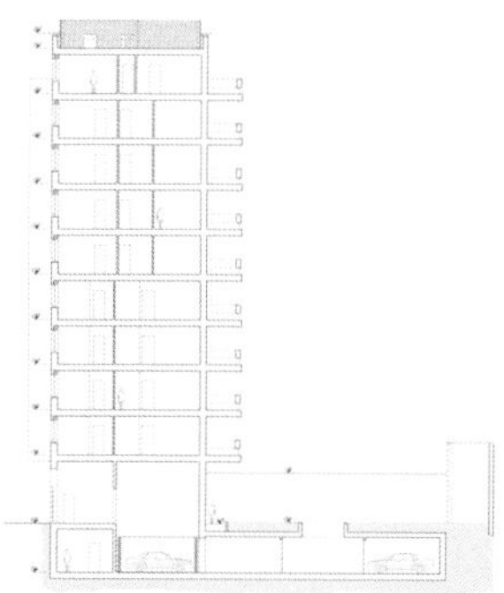

Typical floor layout

Building section

Ground floor view

Front view of facade with spacious loggias

29 **Residenze Montegani**
Via Montegani

Piuarch

This project involves the recovery of a building built around a courtyard in Via Montegani 14 to create apartments in the centre of a residential area in Milan undergoing total redevelopment. The relationship between the new construction and the nature of the existing building is the key to the whole project. From the composition of the façade, the attention to the link between past and present is immediately obvious. This is especially true for the southern aspect that has been raised by two floors over the rest of the reconstruction, but is perceived as a continuous part of the internal facades, creating a dialogue between the new and existing buildings.

The project concept was based on an analysis of the living space, openings and connecting areas. The internal courtyard was redefined by replacing the old facade with a new concept, designed with large openings, in contrast with the external facades clad in terracotta. The layout of the apartments was based on an in-depth analysis of the living space and reveals a basic concept that brings strong personality to the new areas, once again proposing a formal contrast with the existing building.

The 102 apartment units are spread over four stairwells, one pre-existing and three to be newly constructed. Their location in the corners of the building leaves the internal facades free for large openings and provides considerable flexibility for apartment layout on each floor, as well as simplifying the structural system.
V.M.

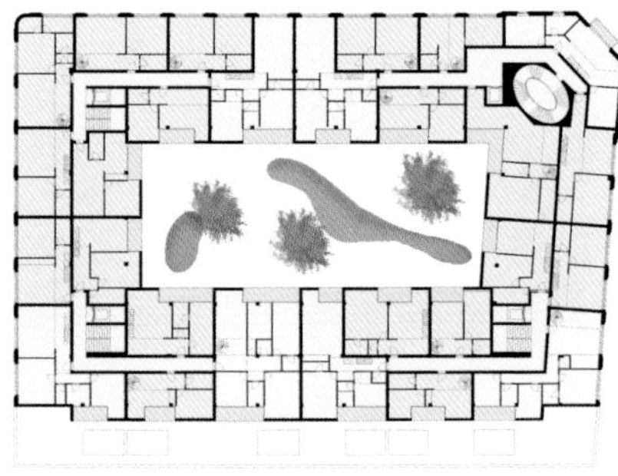

Existing external front facade

First floor layout

Apartment internal view

New intervention overlooking internal courtyard

30 La Forgiatura
Via Varesina

Giuseppe Tortato

The redevelopment of the Forgiatura is a reclamation project to recover a decommissioned industrial area north-west of Milan in the Certosa area.

The project is composed of seven buildings connected to one another through a system of pathways, gardens and artificial hills. The green areas are an integrated part of the complex, as is the sustainability concept of the whole intervention, with the use of hydrothermal systems (geothermal energy) rainwater recovery, integrated solar panel roofing and led lighting systems. All equipment and technical systems are concealed in the artificial hills accessed by an underground pedestrian technological tunnel that connects the various buildings. La Forgiatura was conceived as a contemporary complex that has maintained its strong ties with the industrial plant's past history, but at the same time, its flexible design makes it accessible and open to a range of different destinations. From this perspective, each structure features specific architectural aspects that are distinct from one another. Facing the street is the new eight story "Raimondi" building, covering 10,000 square metres, while in the internal site, the other six buildings have maintained their original structures, with slight changes to facades for better flow and access. On the Office Building, a cantilevered architectural element was added to the top floor; the asymmetrical position forms an imposing projection over the main entrance in Via Varesina. Within the Tempra and Forgia buildings — that have strong historical ties with the former steel industry and have been completely restored and renovated — a large patio area has been created to connect.
C.G.

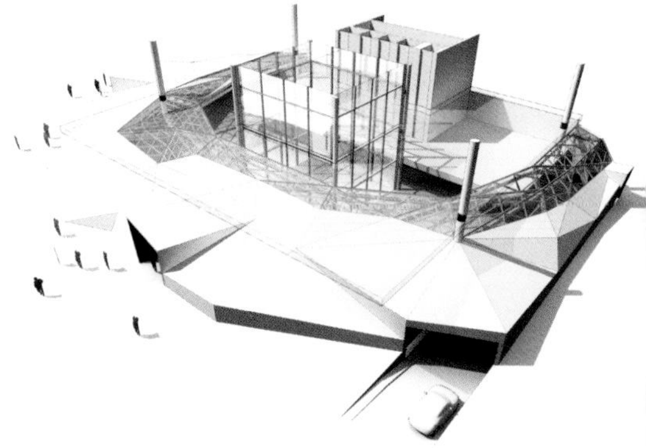

Three-dimensional cross-section study of the Raimondi hill

Aerial photo of the Forgiatura before the intervention with a realistic simulation of the area after regeneration

The Starship and the Raimondi building seen from the terrace of the Uffici building

The Uffici building "framed" by the Meccanica portico and the photovoltaic roof

Greater Milan

31. Cascina Merlata – Expo Village
Via Capo Rizzuto

32. Milanofiori Nord
Assago (Milan)

33. Daisaku Ikeda New Cultural Centre for Peace
Via Marchesi, Corsico (Milan)

34. New Holding Humanitas Offices
Rozzano (Milan)

35. "Vittorio Sereni" Municipal Library
Via Agnese Pasta, Melzo (Milan)

36. MedaTeca New Meda Municipal Library
Via Gagarin, Meda (Monza e Brianza)

37. Music Centre
Cassano d'Adda (Milan)

38. House in the plains
Gropello Cairoli (Pavia)

31 **Cascina Merlata – Expo Village**
Via Capo Rizzuto

Antonio Citterio Patricia Viel and Partners, Caputo Partnership, MCA Mario Cucinella Architects, Teknoarch, CZA Cino Zucchi Architetti, C+S Associati, Pura, B22

On the main north-west Milan highway, near the Expo site and the Rho-Pero fair grounds, the EuroMilano Company is promoting the construction of an innovative metropolitan housing complex in the Cascina Merlata area based on advanced principles of environmental sustainability.

Following a competition launched in 2008 by CascinaMerlata S.p.A. to draw up a planimetric/volumetric project of the area, three winners were declared ex aequo: the firms of Antonio Citterio Patricia Viel and Partners, Caputo Partnership, and MCA Mario Cucinella Architects. To the first two firms, CascinaMerlata S.p.A. assigned the task of drafting the integrated intervention plan.

Other architects are working on the building projects. In particular, the part involving the social housing project (690 apartments) was designed by Cino Zucchi Architetti, C+S Associati, MCA Mario Cucinella Architects, Teknoarch, B22 and Pura. The latter are a group of architects under 30 who recently won awards in the AAA Architetticercasi contests. As well as the residential concept, this new urban district includes the construction of a range of services such as schools (two kindergartens, a pre-school, a primary school and middle school), public spaces to include five recreational parks, and the renovation of the cascina farm buildings for functions for the local population. Later, the Expo 2015 Village will also be reconverted back to residential use with local services. In addition, a large shopping mall and local shops will be built along the avenue that crosses the quarter from north to south. A vast park that will act as a connecting element among the various areas will become the heart of this intervention. The renovated cascina will be used to host functions of public interest and will also house a medical centre. The courtyard represents the pedestrian and cycling "gateway" to Expo.

80% of the public works of the entire Cascina Merlata area will be completed by 2015, including the infrastructures, services and most of the public park areas. From May, the Expo Village will house more than 1,334 delegates from the countries participating at Expo 2015. It is composed of 7 residential towers, designed by the firms Mario Cucinella Architects (3 towers), Teknoarch (2 towers), B22 (1 tower) and Pura (1 tower), containing a total of 397 apartments for a surface of about 30,500 square metres. After the conclusion of the Expo Fair, alongside the first towers, four further buildings will be built beginning in July 2016. These were designed CZA Cino Zucchi Architetti, and C+S Associati, and will house 293 apartments with a total surface of 21,000 square metres. In order to assess the daily needs of the Expo Village, research was carried out in collaboration with Politecnico of Milan, who carried out an international survey for the interior design, the definition of the living space and the choice of furnishings. These plans were developed keeping in mind two types of use: the temporary phase during the months of the Expo Fair, and the permanent use in the following period. The project for the interiors of the domestic units in the Village includes the possibility of reusing the furnishings and finishes.

The creation of this district has focussed particular attention on the questions linked with environmental sustainability applied to all levels of the project. Cascina Merlata will be the first zero emission housing district. This social housing project has foreseen energy class A buildings with the application of geothermal systems supported by heat exchanger pumps and solar panels, as well as district heating and gas free systems.
A.M./M.G.M.

Pre-existent farm buildings

The Cascina Merlata buildings created for Expo 2015

Area Masterplan

previous page, above
MCA apartment buildings by Mario Cucinella Architects

previous page, below right
Building designed by B22

previous page, below left
The competition for the school complex was won by Onsite Studio

Building designed by Pura

32 **Milanofiori Nord**
Assago (Milan)

Masterplan Designed by Erick van Egeraat

Milanofiori Nord is a new multifunctional urban district nearing completion that has been under development in recent years in the Comune of Assago (south of Milan). This refined project is closely linked with the protected agricultural and rural area of Parco Sud. The Master plan designed by the Dutch architect Erick van Egeraat has integrated the pre-existing wooded areas with commercial, residential and service industry zones in a project that enhances and respects the biodiversity of the territory combining architecture and nature in the same context.

The project covers a triangular portion of the area. The side that is bordered by the Milan-Genoa motorway is occupied by a row of administrative buildings that perform a communication and identity function and act as a visual and acoustic filter between the motorway and the internal area destined for residential buildings.

The first stage of the intervention involved the construction of the buildings designed by Erick van Egeraat destined for community and recreational activities, arranged around an urban piazza. It entailed the construction of over 120,000 square metres of office buildings facing the motorway, residential and commercial buildings, and shopping malls (by the architectural studio 5+1AA Alfonso Femia Gianluca Peluffo). It was completed in 2010, with the handover of the independent residences designed by OBR. The residential complex, based on strong sustainable and eco-compatible principles, was the winner of the LEAF architectural award (Leading European Architects Forum) 2011, in the "Best residential building" category, and won the Overall Winner Award among all the projects that took part in the LEAF Awards.

The second stage involved the completion of the iconic U15 building, clad in golden brise-soleil slats, designed by CZA, in 2011.

In July 2012, the last subsidised residential buildings were completed (designed by ABDA). This building houses forty-seven apartments with compact vertical cladding on the northern and southern facades, while the other two sides feature open balconies.

The final intervention is the new service industry building designed Park Associati, for Nestlé Italiana S.p.A. and completed in January 2014. The building is based on an articulated system conceived like a campus; in spite of being constructed around an enclosed courtyard, it provides extensive views between the various elements and the spaces around the complex. The building is connected with the surrounding green areas thanks to the fragmented composition conceived like "suspended boxes" of varying heights and dimensions. Strong focus was placed on the aspects concerning energy saving and low consumption earning the building Gold Class "Core and Shell" Leed certification.
A.M.

U15 Office buildings,
CZA Cino Zucchi Architetti

above
Milanofiori Nord sector, masterplan Designed by Erick van Egeraat

below
Independent residential buildings, OBR Open Building Research

left
Subsidised apartment buildings, ABDArchitetti Botticini De Appolonia e Associati

right
U27 Office building, Park Associati

33 **Daisaku Ikeda New Cultural Centre for Peace**

Via Marchesi, Corsico (Milan)

Peia Associati Srl - Giampiero Peia, Marta Nasazzi

The architectural project for the largest Buddhist centre in Europe is a contrast between the contemporary expression of the new intervention, and the sobriety of the conservation restoration of the historical structure. Set beside each other along the main axis, the farmstead and the country villa are visually connected to the heart of the new building: the sacred scroll (Gohonzon) is enclosed in a shrine (butsuma), inside the jewel box (butsudan) prayer hall; the hall is clad in a golden coloured metal skin and is posed on a mirror of water.

The source of inspiration for the large prayer hall/auditorium is the golden carp, which in the traditional Japanese iconography represents courage, determination and transformation.

The final form is the result of the mediation between the initial project concept and the research carried out to reduce the impact of volume and energy consumption in order to obtain maximum energy performance inside the prayer hall and achieve the best visual and perceptive relationship with the altar (shumidan).

The glassed foyer, a completely white space that captures the light, acts as a filter between the landscape, the view of the cherry tree garden and the large hall, introducing the bridges and glassed passageways that cross the reflecting pool.

The restoration of the historical structure complex has maintained the existing layout practically unchanged, integrating it with strongly incisive architectural interventions. This has maintained the historical and rural nature of the buildings as far as possible with the recovery of fragments of internal and external decoration.
D.S.

Nocturnal view of the Centre with illuminated foyer

View of the facade towards the street with the large golden "jewel box" mirrored in the reflection pool

Internal centre space

34 **New Holding Humanitas Offices**
Rozzano (Milan)

FTA | Filippo Taidelli Architetto

This project involved the restructuring of an existing building in disuse within the hospital complex of the Istituto Clinico Humanitas in Rozzano. It was renovated to create the new management headquarters and a landmark symbol for Humanitas.

The building now has a solid parallelepiped form, balanced on the edge of a large roofed area devoid of any entrance to the main building.

The aim of the project takes advantage of this privileged position to generate a kind of light box, a translucent volume that projects great transparency and clarity from the interior and provides strong visible impact when seen from the road when it is lit up at night.

The connection with the convalescent wing opposite is created by a new roof system that is covered with a roof garden and large planters that can be enjoyed by visitors and can be overlooked by convalescing patients from their windows.

Within a wider urban planning project for greater Milan, FTA is studying a project for the construction of a research campus for the Istituto Clinico Humanitas, again in Rozzano. The university structure, integrated within a larger infrastructural project, will provide services and space for a thousand students.
V.M.

Nocturnal view of the Humanitas Holding Office building

View of the office building overlooking the garden

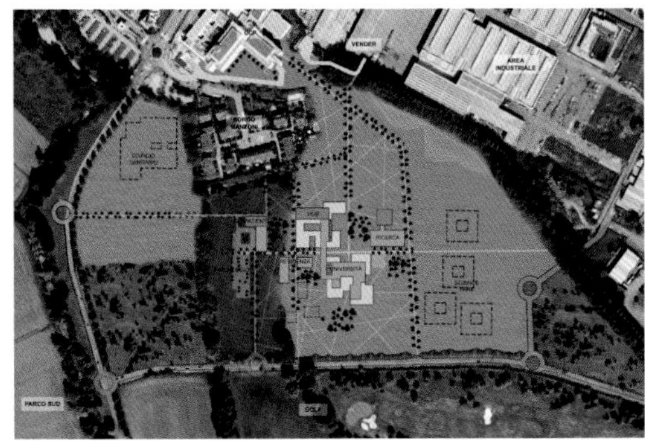

Masterplan of the research campus at the Istituto Clinico Humanitas

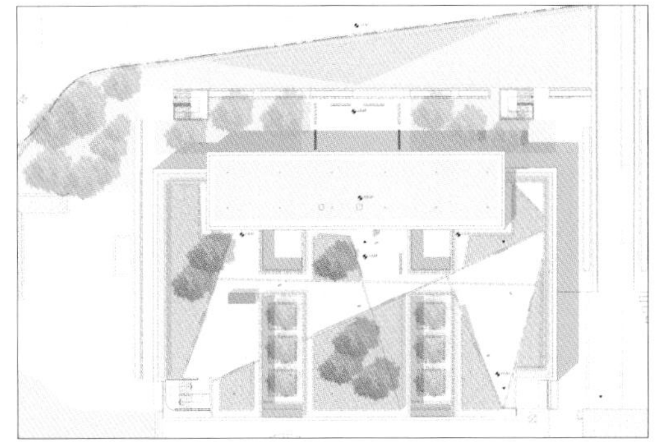

Humanitas Holding Office layout

35 **"Vittorio Sereni" Municipal Library**
Via Agnese Pasta, Melzo (Milan)

Alterstudio Partners

This project by Alterstudio Partners in the historical centre of Melzo fulfils all the traditional library needs for study and information but associates them with an innovative concept of social-cultural integration. The aim is to make the new library a pleasant meeting place for spending time together.

Internally, the staggered levels and large windows overlooking the internal courtyards provide a contemporary interpretation of the traditional style of library buildings, with a welcoming light and airy architectural design.

The "piazza della cultura" (cultural meeting place) faces Via Agnese Pasta and the parvis of the former church of Sant'Andrea, where the pavement design composed of porphyry blocks continues inside the library building to accentuate the flow from exterior to interior. This helps create the atmosphere of a covered piazza in the library entrance foyer, to emphasise the sense of a meeting place for the local population. This area houses the reception and information desks, a café, current exhibitions and the newspaper reading room. The large central staircase overlooks the internal courtyard through a glass wall, and connects the various sections of the library in a staggered floor level layout.

The attention paid to the needs of those who use the library have made this project a true "home for readers". The study and research area with well-equipped workspaces, sits alongside the two floors of the Fiction and Non-fiction section, and a reading area with a range of different designer armchairs. The upper level is dedicated to Children and Young People, a space also created for family leisure time, where a special room for tiny children has also been included. Lastly, the section dedicated to Music, performance and recreation is located in the basement and opens out onto a sunken courtyard with plant-covered walls. Customised furniture blends with designer items, and in the background are the large windows and walls decorated by renowned Italian illustrators like Chiara Armellini, Silvia Bonanni, Gaia Stella De Sanguine, Ilaria Faccioli, Alessandro Sanna, and Valerio Vidali.

This building project had to deal with strong urbanistic restrictions in the historical centre, but the final effect shows a building that blends harmoniously in the surrounding context while maintaining its decidedly contemporary style. The large glassed openings deconstruct the more enclosed concept of study environments and act to maintain the strong connection between interior and exterior. The titanium-zinc cladding envelopes the whole building extending to become part of the roof and façade.

This class A building uses heating pumps fed by groundwater that guarantees a 76% abatement in energy consumption for heating and cooling systems.
C.G.

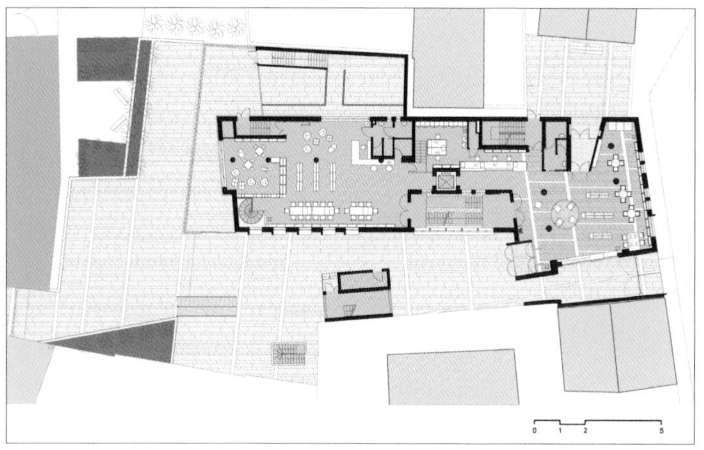

Ground floor layout

External view of the new building

Nocturnal view of the building

Section of the library

BIBLIOTECA

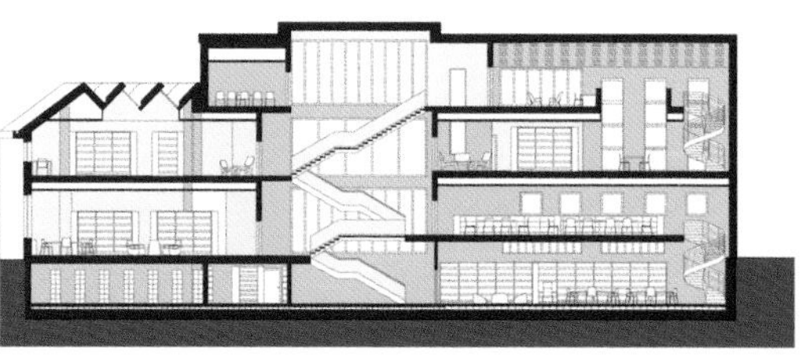

36 **MedaTeca**

New Meda Municipal Library

Via Gagarin, Meda (Monza e Brianza)

Alterstudio Partners

The MedaTeca, a 1,900 square metre building in the centre of Meda redefines the concept of the public library, interpreted as "piazza della cultura" (cultural meeting place) for the town and territory and a "social catalyser" for the local community.

The project involved the recovery of a pre-existing two storeyed building, reinventing the external shell according to the internal content, increasing the volume, modifying the facades, and changing the morphological and material characteristics.

The front facade design, materials and colours, with large windows that overlook the street showing the interior of the building or shaded with semi-transparent coloured blinds, combine to reinforce the library's new function as an "urban condenser".

The facades are clad in Bordeaux aluminium panels (each sheet customised and different in size) arranged in an irregular pattern to encase the window openings; large double height windows overlook the street and a bow-window structure provides impact on the side façade.

The ground and basement floors form the entrance and reception area; the section for children and young people is on the first floor with a long ribbon window overlooking the street; the second and third floors house the open shelf sections, arranged around a double height space lit by a zenith skylight. On the second basement floor is a multi-functional space, a lecture room, and two storerooms. The first basement floor has a study room, a work help desk, and a meeting room. There is also a roof terrace where a small coffee bar will be installed.

The internal layout has been designed with maximum flexibility (for both logistics as well as installations) and each floor, including the study room and terrace can be opened independently for easy access even when the rest of the building is closed.

The inside spaces are large, well lit and comfortable: double-height rooms with open balcony views from one floor to another create a kind of "vertical piazza". In the centre of the building is a skylight that provides daylight for the double height central space of the open shelf section (second and third floors).

The large, double height windows overlooking the street are punctuated with vertical brise-soleil panels and coloured internal sunblinds that provide views of the interior from outside.

Great attention has been paid to domotics and energy saving, both for the heating and lighting systems (low consumption lighting and heat pumps) as well as for the facades, designed and engineered to provide high performance acoustic and thermal insulation.
M.G.M.

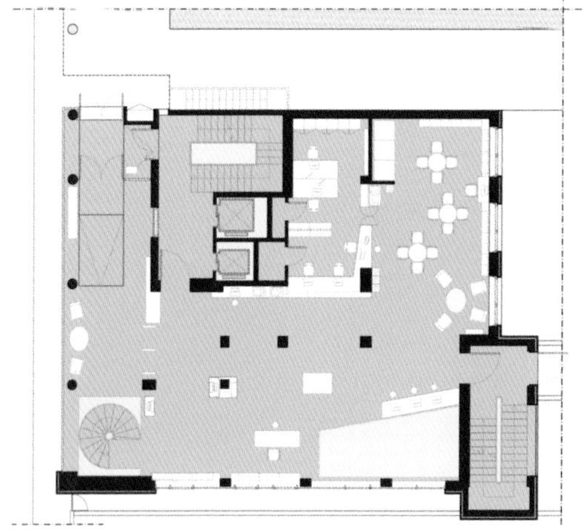

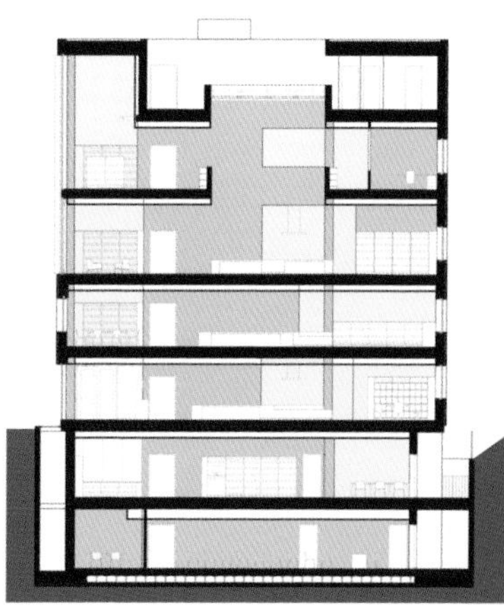

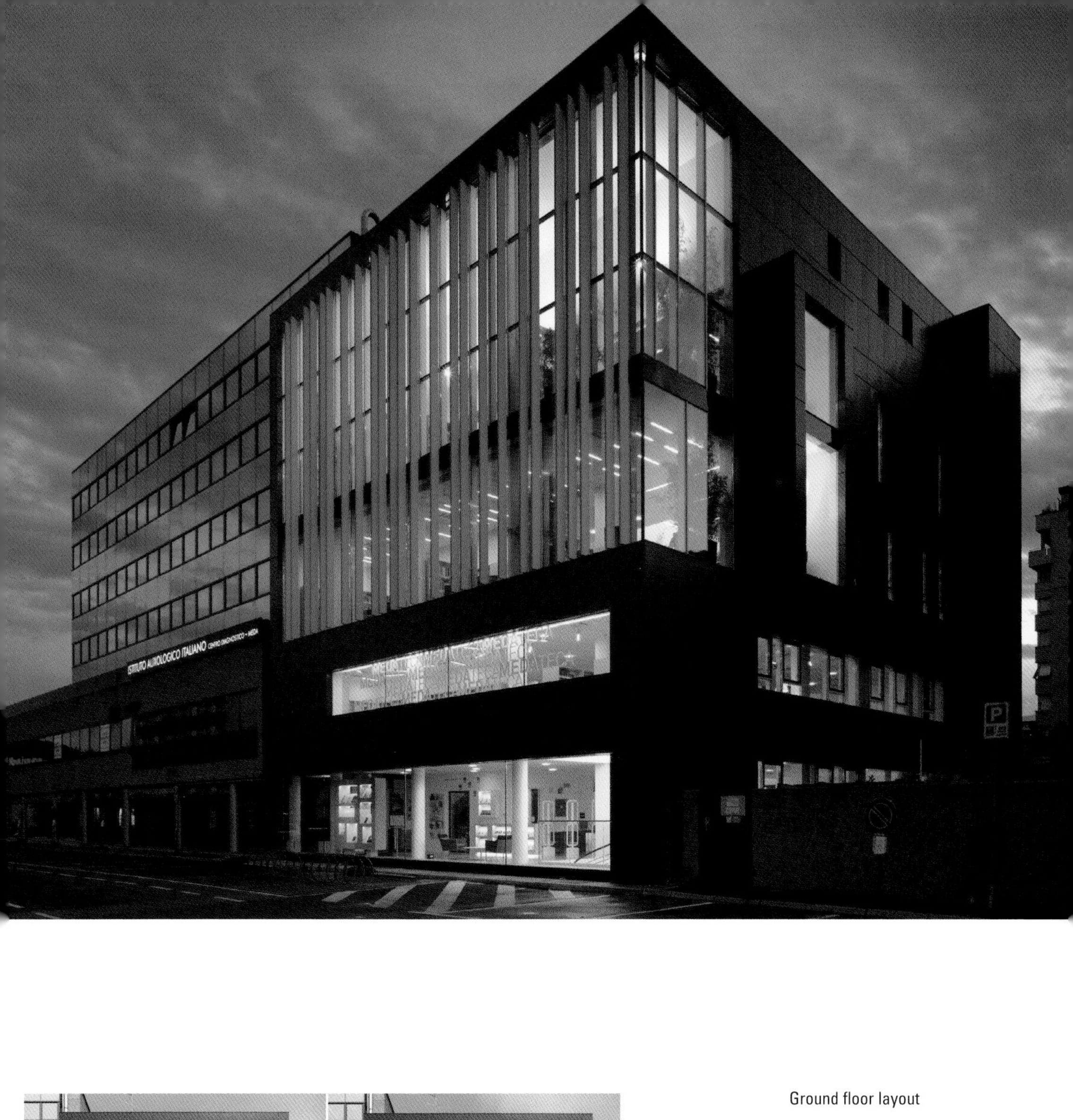

Ground floor layout

Section of the building

External view

Vertical brise-soleil system and coloured internal blinds

37 **Music Centre**
Cassano d'Adda (Milan)

DAP Studio / Elena Sacco, Paolo Danelli

A centre dedicated completely to music based on the design of the Milanese firm, DAP STUDIO, will soon be completed in the historical town of Cassano d'Adda, only a few kilometres from Milan. The music centre, which will be achieved in 2015, will include an auditorium with seating for 3,000, the Municipal Music School, a café, bookshop, and services.

The project also includes redevelopment of the surrounding spaces, the external areas, green spaces and parking, to provide a complete and unified transformation of the zone.

The centre is a compact building with three storeys above ground and one basement floor. The facade has been clad using a material that emphasises the volume and form: press formed perforated white aluminium sheets. The outer skin encloses the whole perimeter of the building, projects over certain window openings and protects the patios on the second floor. On the ground floor, the aluminium sheeting is interrupted to create an open space for a vast glassed area that welcomes the public and creates a strong visual impact between the internal foyer and the piazza.

The compact external aspect contrasts with the dynamic layout of the internal spaces: there is a strong interconnection among the various levels, projecting volumes, overhead walkways and circuits in total height spaces.

The foyer, and heart of the building, forms a large internal piazza that rises for three floors: this will host events, exhibitions and concerts. This large hollow space places the other activities of the Centre in physical and visual contact: the auditorium on one side, the bookshop area and office spaces on the other.

The Music school is located on the second floor. The classrooms, of various sizes, are arranged along the perimeter, alternating with the patios that bring fresh air and natural light into the building and punctuate the internal volume.

Service facilities are located in the basement floor: public bathroom, storerooms, cupboard storage, technical service rooms, and the workshop for the auditorium.

A.M.

Ground floor layout

Central foyer section

External view of uniform facade with aluminium sheet cladding

View of interior with multiple volumes and double height ceilings

38 **House in the plains**
Gropello Cairoli (Pavia)

deamicisarchitetti

This house is set in a quiet suburb located on the outskirts of the town, yet at the same time refuses to comply with the neutral housing styles in the surrounding area. This project by the Deamicis architetti firm, breaks away from rigid parcelling plan principles and the construction is built right on the edge of the property. The building spreads out towards the road, generating spaces of different styles within its confines and urban aspects with specific identity and character.

The northern side, which is closest to the road, shows the urban facade of the house, with an access parvis paved in serpentine stone. Continuing along the front of the house is a pergola that protects the facade and the building gradually opens out onto the garden with large windows filtered by perforated corten screens. The garden blends with the internal spaces, designed to facilitate a direct relationship with the green garden space through a series of changing views. Another green space, 5-metres deep (measurements imposed by regulations), slopes down to meet the planted enclosure to create a background landscape to be viewed from inside the home.

The project recalls traditional old farmhouses with their large overhanging roofs. In fact, the house is dominated by the roof that slopes to accommodate the changing facades, also becoming an integrated part of the facade as well and defining the front aspect that faces the neighbouring houses.

The interior layout follows the pattern of traditional farmhouses with a sequence of rooms that follow on without any further additions. The plain simple materials are used extensively. The interior features large glass partitions, wooden furniture, and oak and marble terrazzo flooring; white plaster and black tiles make a striking contrast on external walls.
A.M.

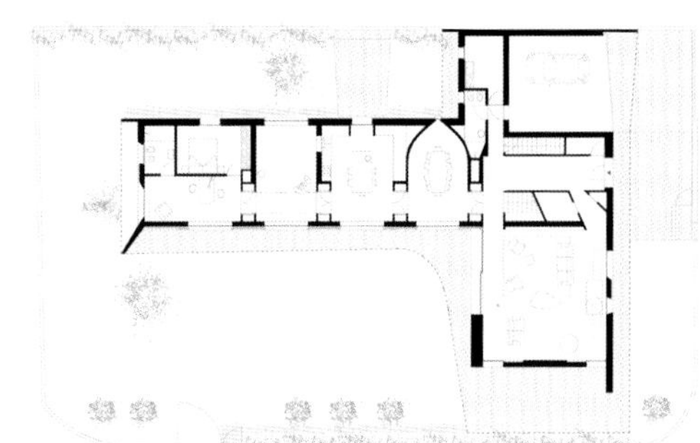

Project layout

View of external facade
towards the street

The roof descends to cover
the entire side of the building
on the facade opposite
neighbouring houses

P&I

*Susanna Legrenzi**

Expo Milano 2015, the construction site at a glance

The (physical) access to construction sites is controlled by a long series of rules and regulations. Making a huge public works site (visually) accessible is an operation based on transparency. To translate this principle into reality, a physics observatory would be necessary, and in this case, given the surface of the area, it would need to be as tall as a construction crane. The alternative would be to design a narration communication system using new media methods. When this question was raised in Expo Milano 2015, the objective that I shared as Head of Social Media Strategy, was to guarantee (digital) access to the construction site; this was to be constant over time and as widespread as possible, focussing not only on photography, but also on new technologies: on one hand, the drones, and on the other, ultra-fast connectivity. The result was "Belvedere in città" (Belvedere in the city). The figures: more than thirty drone flights per week over the construction site, shared under Creative Commons license. The project was created in co-design with TIM, Official World Fair Global Partner, which made all its technological capabilities available. Thanks to TIM 4G, the technology that provides mobile navigation with ultra-fast connection, the over-flights were able to record all the work completion phases with an extremely high picture quality: Ultra HD (4K Ultra High Definition). In line with Italian regulations, the flights (controlled by certified pilots and performed during the lunch break) were carried out for TIM by operators from an ENAC registered company. Equipped with six electric high-power motors with on-board electronics able to maintain the drones stable even under bad weather conditions, the filming drones were equipped with a GPS system, infrared sensors, and other environmental characteristic detection systems. Thanks to this filming, both the videos and all the iconographic materials have been recorded in high definition. Available between September 2014 and April 2015, "Belvedere in città" has been an observation point open to millions of users. On the Milan Expo you-tube channel alone, "Belvedere in città" has had an average of twenty thousand viewings for each episode; the Facebook page has had a reach of over three hundred thousand impressions per video. The films have been used several times in television programs, projected for public presentations, shared with participating countries and other international stakeholders. "Belvedere in città" has been the first international project to date to have constantly documented the work in progress of a construction site for over six months. The passage from the first filming performed in September to the final shots is like a single panorama, able to convey a true idea of the enormous commitment by more than 4000 operators, working seven days a week, on a construction site of over one million square metres in size.

*Head of Social Media Strategy Expo 2015 (October 2014 - February 2015)

Expo 2015

The site chosen to host the 2015 World's Fair is located in the north-west sector of the Milan metropolitan area and continues along the axis of Corso Sempione. The area is circumscribed by a network of important major roads that form the Expo boundaries enclosing the site, and by a canal that has been included in the redevelopment project as one of the cardinal elements of this "extraordinary landscape".

The physical concept introduced by five architects of international renown (Jacques Herzog, Richard Burdett, Stefano Boeri, Joan Busquets and William A. McDonough) was aimed at representing the main theme of the fair itself — "Feeding the Planet, Energy for Life" and in defining a landscape that is both multicultural and multicultivational.

In fact, the project was conceived like a vast park to inspire intervention, not only by the organising body, but also by the countries involved in the Exposition. Together with the governing council, the Expo 2015 S.p.A. team developed a project based on four fundamental principles: strong focus on the main theme, prominence given to the participant countries, landscape quality, and sustainability.

This final element was a fundamental feature in the master plan development, which, like the central concept is based on the idea of rational and intelligent use of the raw materials of our planet: water, earth, sun, plant life, climate... With this in mind, regulations were established for all participants to ensure that pavilion construction was truly sustainable, with reduced energy consumption during construction as well as during pavilion use, using sustainable materials that could be recycled.

The temporary structures, including the various service buildings, were the object of a recent international project contest, won by an Italian team (Onesitestudio, A. Liverani, E. Molteni, M. Lavagna, L.C. Tagliabue, M. Buzzetti).

They had to be sustainable for their entire work life, in accordance with the "light touch" approach where no traces remain on the site after the closure of the event, and with minimum impact on the environment.

In line with the same sustainability principles, Expo adheres to the LEED for Neighbourhood protocol. Numerous calls for competitive bids were announced, followed by further bids for these projects.

As far as the individual pavilions are concerned, each country managed the project design of its own exhibition space independently. Two main axes form the basic master plan grid matrix: the Decumanus runs from the centre towards the boundaries symbolically linking the food consumption areas (urban zones) with those where the food is produced (rural zones).

The Cardo runs perpendicular to the first axis forming the unifying element with the peripheral ring of park spaces and green structures that are linked with one another enclosing the site.

The participant country pavilions are located every twenty metres along the Decumanus; each country was able to choose to build its own pavilion, or to opt for a cluster solution composed of several representatives in a combined space. The shorter axis — the Cardo — is surrounded by exhibition spaces and food tasting areas hosted by participant countries. At one end of the Cardo, close to the Lake Arena, is Palazzo Italia, the official meeting place for the host country and participants.

Built on three raised floors above ground level, the area underneath forms a vast covered piazza destined for events. At the intersection point between the Cardo and the Decumanus is another large piazza. The canal that surrounds the Expo site is an element of primary importance. Firstly because of its strong thematic connection with the traditional Milanese Naviglio canal system and secondly for its technical function for site irrigation and microclimate control.

The service buildings are located at regular intervals within the orthogonal grid along the Decumanus, in the main public areas, and along the perimeter paths. The green areas and the walkways near the service areas create zones for relaxing. With the canal, the main iconic elements of the Expo site mark the landscape in the cardinal points: the Mediterranean Hill, the Open Air Theatre, the Lake Arena and the Expo Centre.

As well as acting as reference points within the Expo site for visitors, these elements are also destined to host the major events during the Fair. The most visible is the Tree of Life, the towering symbol (37 metres) of the Italian Pavilion, created by Marco Balich, the pavilion's artistic director and producer of famous international events. The 22-metre high Hill representing

the Mediterranean agricultural ecosystem is another main landmark. Designed to be accessible to all visitors, it includes a ramp system that leads visitors to the top of the hill to enjoy the impressive views.

The Open Air Theatre, located in the southern part of the Expo area, can seat around nine thousand spectators on lawn areas and tiered bench seating for open-air concerts, theatrical performances and official ceremonies. The Lake Arena, fed from the canal, is a vast pool surrounded by tiered seating for three thousand spectators, or standing space for six thousand. The pool will host performances on the water, artistic installation exhibitions and temporary events.

At the far end of the west side of the Decumanus is the Expo Centre composed of three independent blocks: an auditorium (southern block) performance area (central block) and the office building (northern block). The first two blocks are designed to be dismantled after the conclusion of the fair, while the office building will be a permanent fixture. The awning system, which was one of the main features of the initial concept, now covers all the pedestrian walkways. Business companies have able to participate as theme area suppliers or sponsors, or have been able to create their own space and pavilion in one of the exhibition site areas (such as Intesa Sanpaolo with the aMDL pavilion).

The nine theme areas are spaces designed by the organisers to host events and to house explanatory or entertainment installations based on nutrition, health and wellbeing. The Cascina Triulza, a pre-existent farm complex in traditional Padana Plain style, was restored and redeveloped to exhibit the Best Practices processes linked with the Expo theme; it houses the spaces for the Civil Society and the Centre for Sustainable Development, an avant-garde structure for technological food research that will remain in the city of Milan after the conclusion of Expo 2015.

Expo Milano 2015

39. Arid Zone Cluster
Expo Milano 2015

40. Bio-Mediterraneum Cluster
Expo Milano 2015

41. Cocoa Cluster
Expo Milano 2015

42. Coffee Cluster
Expo Milano 2015

43. Cereals and Tubers Cluster
Expo Milano 2015

44. Fruits and Legumes Cluster
Expo Milano 2015

45. Spices Cluster
Expo Milano 2015

46. Islands, Sea, and Food Cluster
Expo Milano 2015

47. Rice Cluster
Expo Milano 2015

48. Pavilion 0
Expo Milano 2015

49. Italian Pavilion
Expo Milano 2015

50. France Pavilion
Expo Milano 2015

51. United Kingdom Pavilion
Expo Milano 2015

52. Belgium Pavilion
Expo Milano 2015

53. Germany Pavilion
Expo Milano 2015

54. Israel Pavilion
Expo Milano 2015

55. Czech Republic Pavilion
Expo Milano 2015

56. Brazil Pavilion
Expo Milano 2015

57. USA Pavilion
Expo Milano 2015

58. Japan Pavilion
Expo Milano 2015

59. Mexico Pavilion
Expo Milano 2015

60. Chile Pavilion
Expo Milano 2015

61. China Pavilion
Expo Milano 2015

62. Colombia Pavilion
Expo Milano 2015

63. Kuwait Pavilion
Expo Milano 2015

64. Slow Food Pavilion
Expo Milano 2015

65. Intesa Sanpaolo Pavilion
Expo Milano 2015

66. Piacenza Pavilion
Expo Milano 2015

The Clusters

One of the major innovations of this important event is the Cluster system: nine collective thematic pavilions organised according to food categories and production systems. Three are represented according to their environmental aspects — Bio-Mediterraneum, Arid Zones, Islands, Sea and Food — and are located near the Biodiversity Park. The other six are located along the Decumanus and are dedicated to different food categories: fruits and legumes, spices, cereals and tubers, coffee, cocoa and chocolate, and rice, in a widespread and common perspective of the Expo theme: in fact, each cluster has common areas with functional spaces — a market, exhibition displays, performances, food tasting — while each country has its own individual personalised exhibition space. The origin of this initiative is the result of the collaboration between the Polytechnic University of Milan and Expo 2015 during the "Cluster International Workshop", an initiative curated by Matteo Gatto (Director of the Expo 2015 Thematic Areas Sector) and Luisa Collina (Expo Delegate from Polytechnic University of Milan), that produced a vibrant, international, multidisciplinary project plan (architecture, civil engineering and design) developed and then brought to completion by various teams of architects. This resulted in a complex and unprecedented program dealing with a wide range of subjects in a collective process that involved the Polytechnic University of Milan, two other Italian universities, fifteen international universities, a hundred and thirty-five students and over ninety professors and tutors, producing twenty-seven project proposals, three for each of the nine clusters. The results were finally presented at the Expo Milano 2015 International Participants Meeting in October 2012, and a cluster was chosen for each selected field of interest.

[1] "Cluster International Workshop", held between September 19 and October 8, 2012 at the Bovisa Durando campus, Polytechnic University of Milan.

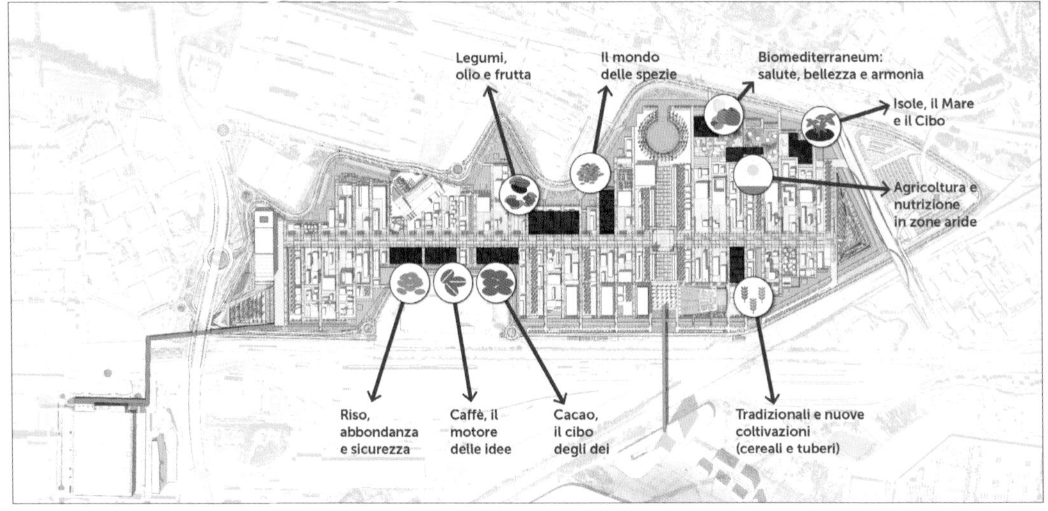

Arid Zone Cluster
Expo Milano 2015

Project coordination: Alessandro Biamonti, Michele Zini. Universities: Politecnico di Milano, Escuela Tecnica Superior de Arquitectura de Madrid (Spagna), Birzeit University (Palestine)

The cluster dedicated to the Arid Zone theme draws its inspiration from sand storms in the desert because of the harsh conditions of living in a territory with environments defined by their lack of water. However, the project wishes to focus attention on the hidden vital resources present in these regions to demonstrate their underlying wealth and richness.

The structure is composed of imposing reticular grid canopy with dozens of semi-transparent tubes suspended overhead to create a nebulous atmosphere of disorientation: inside this space emerge the pavilions and staged decor representing desert rock formations. Set in the midst of the pavilions linked by the grid canopy is a common space destined for events, an opportunity for performances and for gaining deeper knowledge of the subjects on show. The space also includes a market of traditional products grown in the different countries represented within the cluster.

The route through the cluster exhibition spaces begins from the covered open square that links the pavilions. It includes leisure spaces with seating and tables, meeting points, and information panels, to increase the perception of taking a moment's rest, of pausing in an tranquil oasis sheltered from the climatic hardships caused by problems linked with lack of water.
M.T.

40 **Bio-Mediterraneum Cluster**
Expo Milano 2015

Project coordination: Stefano Guidarini, Camillo Magni, Cherubino Gambardella, Lorenzo Capobianco.
Universities: Politecnico di Milano, Seconda Università degli Studi di Napoli, American University in Cairo (Egypt)

The Bio-Mediterraneum Cluster is dedicated to the traditional food culture of the Mediterranean area, an example of maximum interrelation between the value of the food and social customs of the various populations whose countries all border the same stretch of common sea; customs and traditions that have been influenced by centuries of encounter, exchange and integration. The general perception of the Mediterranean almost always recalls total involvement of the all senses in an intermingling of colours, sounds, flavours and aromas.

The project features a vast partially covered central square surrounded by the exhibition pavilions of the various participant countries. The chromatic choices echo the colours of traditional Mediterranean coastal towns in contrast with the harmonious range of sea-blues for the flooring and the white translucent roof coverings representing sails unfurled in the wind over the central area of the cluster.

This area houses the structures dedicated to the sale of traditional food products, open-air kitchens for greater enjoyment of the central space, and to hosting events. These activities are linked with the culture of Mediterranean food to complement the exhibition circuit that is divided according to three main subjects: the history of the Mediterranean — a story narrated through image, literature and film.

M.T.

Cocoa Cluster
Expo Milano 2015

Project coordination: Fabrizio Leoni, Mauricio Cardenas, Cesare Ventura. Universities: Politecnico di Milano, ITESEM - Tecnologico de Monterrey (Mexico), SUPSI Lugano (Switzerland)

The Cluster project dedicated to Cocoa and Chocolate is focussed on evoking the atmosphere of the countries where the cocoa bean is grown, recalling tropical and sub-tropical plantations and the jungle. Stylised branched columns of different shapes and heights symbolise forest trees. The dominant tones are soft warm browns recalling the colours of the cocoa bean. The absence of any roof covering provides direct light diffusion filtered only by the vertical elements, to evoke the effect of dappled light in the jungle.

The pavilions are similar in design and concept and are defined by facades in light semi-transparent fabrics that allow a glimpse of the internal claddings. With explanatory panels, the exhibition circuit leads the visitor through the story of the cocoa bean revealing all the production processing stages. The common spaces that link the exhibition areas follow a main route according to different activities: a zone for relaxing and tasting various cocoa products, an area dedicated to events, and another designed for gastronomic demonstrations.

Careful attention has been paid to the range of different floor finishes; the fan-shaped arrangement of long seating benches facing the performance area and combined with benches and tables in the green space near the Decumano provides leisurely enjoyment and a welcoming perspective to the whole cluster.
M.T.

42

Coffee Cluster Expo Milano 2015

Project coordination: Armando Colombo, Stefan Vieths. Universities: Politecnico di Milano, Fau-Universidade de Sao Paulo (Brazil)

The project for the coffee cluster was inspired by the tropical forests of Africa, Central America and Asia, home to the world's greatest coffee plantations; it was designed to create a setting in which the pavilions represent forest trees covered by a wooden structure that recalls abstract branches overhead.

The composition of the cluster is based on the layout of the exhibition pavilions arranged along a central axis forming a linear piazza covered overhead by wooden slat shade screens, a system that is continued on the wall cladding. The light is filtered through the grids enhancing the warm colours of the internal materials. The exhibition route that links the various pavilions is arranged in five main sections: coffee cultivation greenhouse, transport, bean roasting, café, marketplace, and a meeting place, as well as the external green area where coffee plants grow among the photographic works in the exhibition by Salgado.

The half-covered piazza in the centre creates a series of spaces that can be used by visitors in different ways: the tiered seating for spectators in the events area, tables in the light refreshment area, and the exhibitors' stalls in the marketplace that sell original products linked with coffee production.

M.T.

Cereals and Tubers Cluster
Expo Milano 2015

Project coordination: Alessandro Rocca, Franco Tagliabue. Universities: Politecnico di Milano, Parsons School of Design, New York (USA), MARKHI-Moscow Institute of Architecture (Russia)

The cluster dedicated to cereals and tubers is designed to transmit the essence of traditional cereal cultivation through colour, smell, and architectural finishes.

The project has aligned the exhibition pavilions along a partially covered central axis, to follow a common circuit that expands at one end of the access route to form an open square where the canopy roof forms a kind of large faceted fireplace rising to shelter the restaurant and events area.

The common circuit is developed as a botanical demonstration with a sequence of containers growing a range of different cereals, identified with nameplates and explanatory panels. The objective is to create a combination of information and perception concerning the importance and diffusion of these cereal types.
M.T.

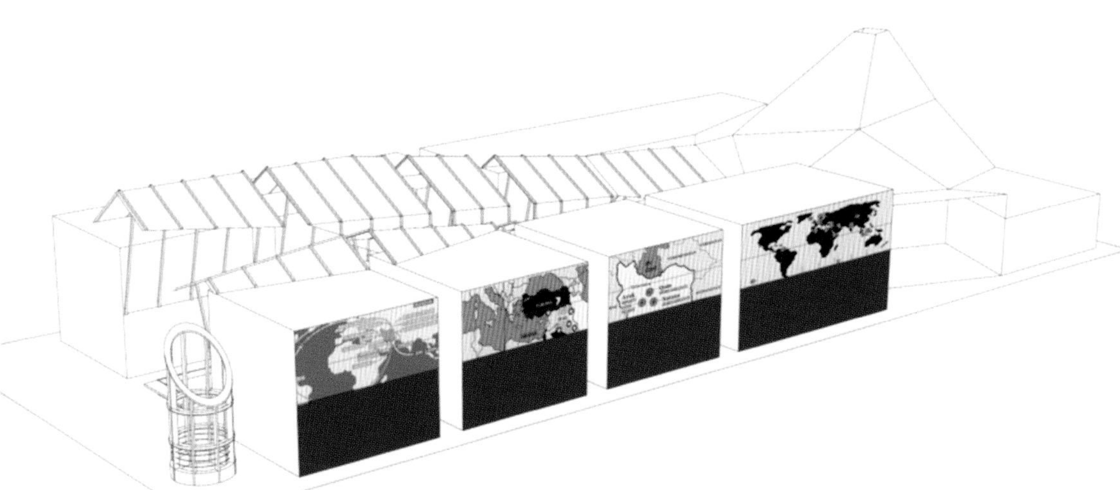

44 Fruits and Legumes Cluster Expo Milano 2015

Project coordination: Massimo Ferrari, Matteo Vercelloni. Universities: Politecnico di Milano, Cape Peninsula University of Technology in Capetown (South Africa), The Bezalel Academy of Art and Design (Israel)

The cluster space for fruit and legumes is designed around a linear central square. An open wooden lattice construction forms the overhead canopy representing a garden pergola that connects the exhibition pavilions arranged in a regular grid form. The pavilion walls are clad in a similar material to create a monochromatic effect with the lattice roof.

The open square houses spaces for events, restaurant areas, information panels and an open fruit market set at the end of the square that communicates with the spice cluster. The spice exhibits are aligned along the length of a partially covered structure. Certain spaces of the common area have been planted with fruit trees and another area opposite the pavilions is planted with legume beds to provide a complete vision of the world of fruit and legumes.

M.T.

Spices Cluster
Expo Milano 2015

Project coordination: Michele Brunello, Pierluigi Salvadeo, Benno Albrecht. Universities: Politecnico di Milano, Università Iuav di Venezia, Nid - National Institute of Design (India)

The project for the Spices Cluster invites the visitor set forth on a journey of all five senses recalling the pioneering explorations of the first ocean voyages that, thanks to their search for the spice routes, led to the discovery of important technological innovations. The common areas display the maps of exploration and geographical discovery, and through the different senses with the taste and smell of spices, decorative staging and events, the cluster aims at creating an interaction between various cultures through the wide variety of different products.

The pavilions are arranged in a regular grid formation emphasised by the canopies over the common areas; open-mesh screens connect the exhibition structures creating a vibrant mosaic of interactive panels, seating, and decorative hanging dividers in a refined combination of colour and materials.
M.T.

46 **Islands, Sea, and Food Cluster**
Expo Milano 2015

Project coordination: Marco Imperadori, Giuliana Iannaccone. Universities: Politecnico di Milano, Aalto University of Helsinky (Finland), University of Tokyo (Japan)

The Islands, Sea, and Food Cluster is designed to create the atmosphere of the islands represented through sound, colour and flavour, with the use of water fountains, gravel paths and wooden decking walkways.

The two main pavilions are set parallel to one another and linked by a common area covered with a suspended bamboo canopy for shade over the gravel paths and water fountains. The upper sections of the pavilions are finished in architectural faceted cladding while the lower half displays quotes from famous writers describing the sea, islands and ocean voyages.

At one end of the common circuit are the areas destined for restaurants and events, created under two portico structures built as extensions to the two pavilions. The interior walls feature projected underwater images that literally immerse the visitor in the biodiversity of the islands represented.

M.T.

Rice Cluster
Expo Milano 2015

Project coordination: Agnese Rebaglio, Davide Crippa, Barbara Di Prete
Universities: Politecnico di Milano, Tongij University Shanghai (China), National University of Civil Engineering, Hanoi (Vietnam)

The project for the Rice Cluster is designed to evoke the sights and smells of the rural rice field landscape. The exhibition communication concept is inspired by the various processes involved in rice growing, where the water in the rice fields hides and at the same time contributes to the growth of this cereal that is the main source of nutrition for over half the world's population.

The rice paddy effect is created with a scenographic layout of botanical plots growing a range of different rice varieties plus reflecting pools multiplied by the mirrored walls of the six pavilions set behind the rice beds. Kiosks for rice tasting are set around the common space, and among the rice beds and water pools are interactive plasma screens with information on rice growing. Visitors can learn about the history of rice, its importance in the sphere of biodiversity, and farming production in the countries that have developed rice-growing techniques.

The project design clearly differentiates the pavilion exhibition area from the interactive space opposite destined for events, while still giving prime importance to rice, the main subject of the entire cluster.
M.T.

The pavilions

There are 53 national pavilions in the Expo area as well as a series of impressive regional and thematic structures; it was decided to present certain projects because of their impact, symbolic content, and sustainability features, since they can be considered in line with the theme, or rather, since they express the themes related to this important international fair with such strong impact during a period of crisis, precarious social-political balance and serious reflection.

48 **Pavilion 0**
Expo Milano 2015

Michele De Lucchi

Pavilion 0, situated at the West entrance of the Expo site, is the complex where the exposition's pivotal theme, "Feeding the Planet, Energy for Life", will be presented.

The structure draws inspiration for the concept from the conformation of the Earth's crust, a portion of which has been symbolically extracted, with its undulating system of various gradients. In particular, the project is characterized by the roof made in a step-shaped design, to finish the building, reminiscent of graphic representations of stratigraphic elevations, made using a series of conical wooden steps that make up the form of the overall design.

The structure stands out for its repeated and symmetrical conoidal elements, consisting of four large cones that are alternated in the same number of smaller sizes to emphasize the sequence of the juxtaposition, sharply interrupted by the outer wall in conjunction with the four perimeter sides. The structural skeleton is composed of an organized system of beams and pillars, whose modularity is mirrored between one half of the pavilion and the other, to optimize construction of the slab. The complex's structure is based on a rectangular plan, with the accesses in the short sides, which take up an area of about 7000 square metres. The theme rooms in the pavilion have an irregular geoidal shape, each one different, due to the slanting roof, in a significant architectural correspondence between interior and exterior.

The exhibition rooms are divided thematically between the different cultural productions of man in relation to the landscape in which he finds himself, industrialism, market, power, infrastructure, storage, giving priority to the concept of identity of a population in relation to the territory with which he relates through culture, society and the environment, the main theme underlying Expo 2015.
M.T.

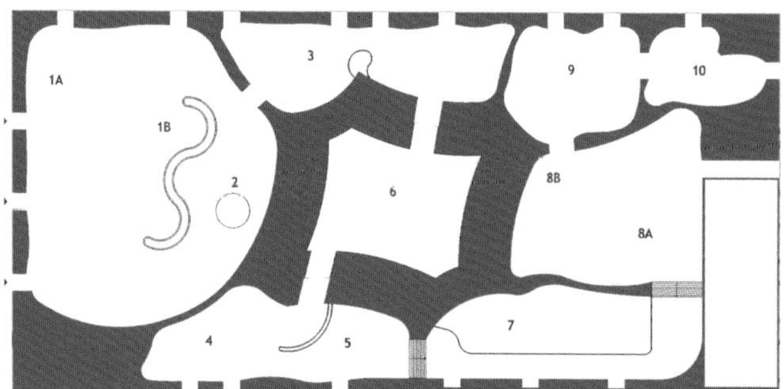

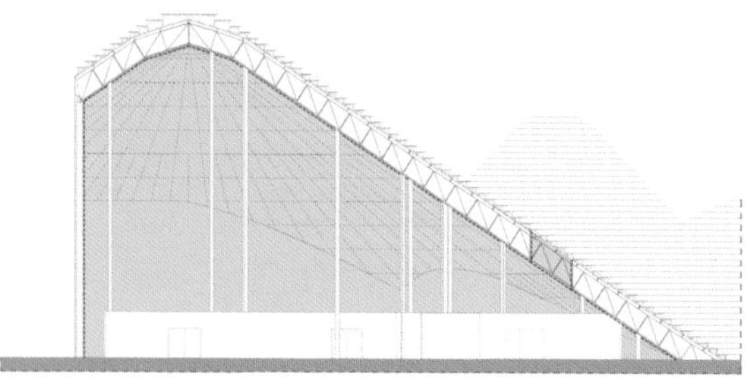

Plan of Pavilion 0 with various sections

Legend
1A. Memory wall
1B. Monitor
2. The tree in the forest
3. Edible substances
4. Tools
5. Containers
6. Valley of civilization
7. Industrialism
8A. The market
8B. Effects of food
9. Landscapes
10. Men and good manners

Section of a cone-shaped roof

The exterior of Pavilion 0

Internal court with the volumes of the different thematically divided exhibition rooms

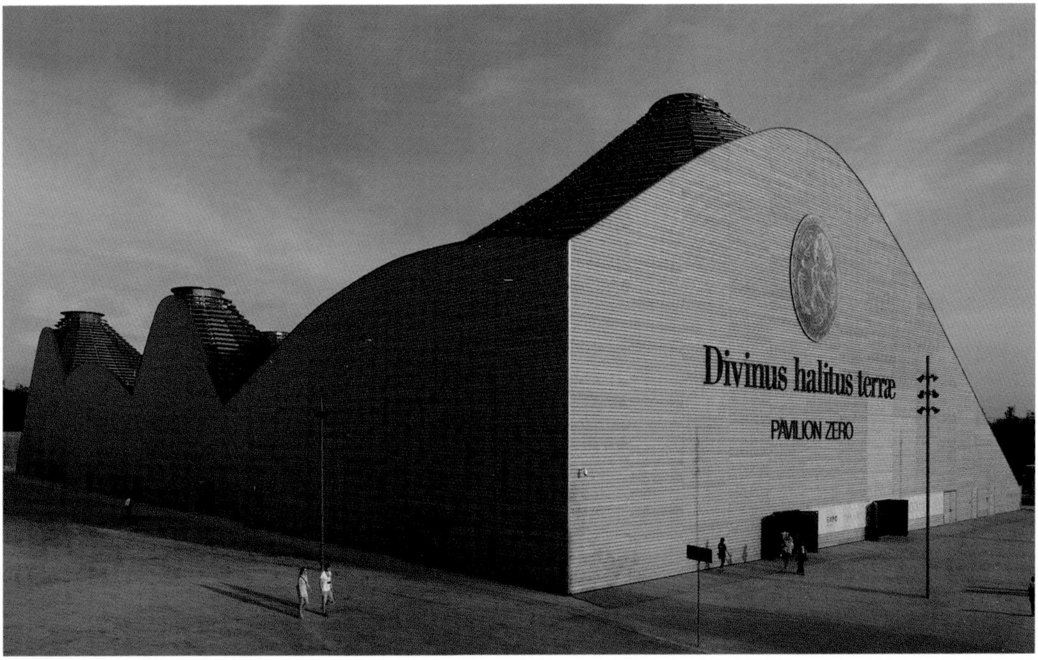
Divinus halitus terræ
PAVILION ZERO

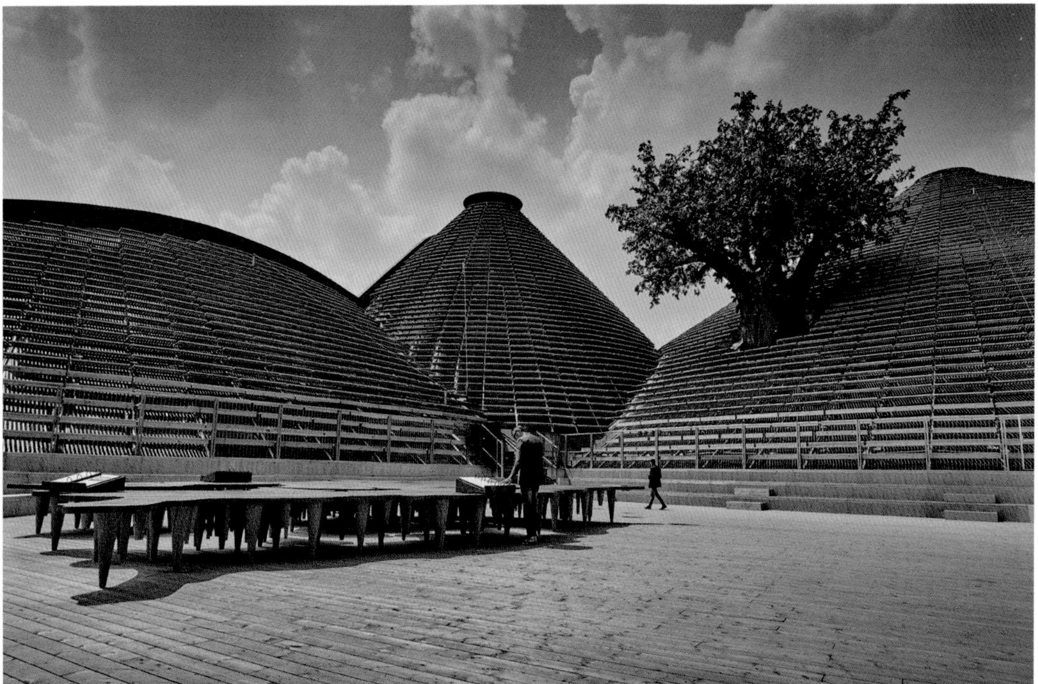

49 Italian Pavilion Expo Milano 2015

Nemesi & Partners

The architecture of Palazzo Italia
Because of its location and architecture, Palazzo Italia assumes the role of landmark within the Expo area: situated on one of the four compass points, to the north, it is the scenic backdrop of the Cardo, the avenue which crosses the exhibition site.

Palazzo Italia was inspired by an "urban forest"; the branching "skin" designed by Studio Nemesi as the building's external envelope evokes a figurativeness that is simultaneously primitive and technological. The weaving of the lines generates alternating light and shadow, voids and filled areas, creating an architecture-sculpture reminiscent of a Land Art work.

For the architecture of Palazzo Italia, the Studio Nemesi started with the idea of cohesion, understood as a force of attraction that generates a renewed sense of community and belonging. The energy of the community is represented by the internal piazza; the symbolic heart and departure point for the exhibition tour, uniting the four volumes that shape Palazzo Italia. These are true urban backdrops. The four blocks respectively host the exhibition (West Block), the Auditorium-Events Area (South Block), the representative offices area (North Block) and the Conference-Meeting Room (East Block). The architectural volumes, metaphors for large trees, have massive ground supports that simulate large roots sinking into the ground. The same volumes, seen from the inner piazza, opening and stretching upwards, free themselves like treetops going through the large glass roof. To make Palazzo Italia's sculptural forms stand out is the rich branching texture of the outer envelope. For the design of this "skin", Nemesi created a unique and original geometric texture that evokes intertwining random branches, creating an architecture within the architecture.

Palazzo Italia was designed to be a sustainable, zero energy building thanks to the contribution of the photovoltaic glass in the roof and the photocatalytic properties of the new concrete for the outer envelope. The roof covering that interprets the image of a forest's canopy of greenery, characterized by mostly quadrangular photovoltaic glass and geometric fields, flat as well as curved, together with the building's branched envelope, is an innovation in both design and technology. The high point of the roof's design is the heart of the inner piazza; a large conical glass skylight is "suspended" above the piazza and central staircase, filling them with natural light.

The Cardo buildings
The temporary buildings of the Cardo, which overlook the thoroughfare of the same name, a paved avenue 35-metres wide and 325-metres long that connects Piazza d'Acqua at the north end to Via d'Acqua at the south end, are designed with a "dry" structural system to be "removed" after the event and relocated elsewhere.

The Nemesi concept for the Cardo buildings is based on the idea of the Italian village, consisting of juxtaposed volumes in small squares, terraces and pathways with porticos. Different geometric compositions, some of them cantilevered, are arranged in succession, fitted together to become a great mosaic in which each piece has its own design autonomy and identity. On the ground floor and first floor are plans for small "piazzas" generated by the alternation of the architectural volumes.

The Cardo buildings will be representative of the Italian territory and particularly the regions. Here they will have their representative and exhibition offices. Facing Palazzo Italia, on the north Cardo, will be some spaces for institutional purposes, exhibitions and offices for the European Union pavilion, symbolically emphasizing the close relationship between Italy and Europe.

The Cardo buildings include: the European Union pavilion, exhibition spaces, event spaces, representation spaces, restaurants, and terraces for events.
D.S.

External view of Palazzo Italia

The internal piazza
with the urban forest

50 **France Pavilion Expo Milano 2015**

XTU Anouk Legendre + Nicolas Desmazières

The design for the French Pavilion at EXPO 2015 recreates a spectacular and "overturned" French landscape. The shape arises from the analysis of the country's territories, the choice that was made thanks to the great variety of places that characterize France; the same territory fostered the growth of a very high quality cultural and gastronomic heritage. With these characteristics, according to the designers, France can start up new farming practices with a new food revolution.

The entire project is designed in "unfinished" wood (the structures, floors and facades), in order to express the great French experience in the construction of wooden frames, in its most "innovative" forms: free forms.

The assemblies are invisible; the highly complex geometry was designed to be digitally cut, thanks to highly advanced technologies that infuse the pavilion with a remarkable architectural quality.

The Pavilion pursues the theme of the Great Market. One room, open to the city, a great roof and the four large pillars supporting it, re-create, thanks to their shade on a hot summer's day, a cool and pleasant environment in which to find shelter.

The challenge was to give tomorrow's market a fresh interpretation, a fertile market, at one time simply a place of exchange, now a place of exchange-production-consumption on the premises. The restaurant, the terrace and the exhibition on the ground floor with the theme "Feeding the world today, feeding the world of tomorrow, the pleasure and the food, the commitment for the future", make the place open, innovative and welcoming.

D.S.

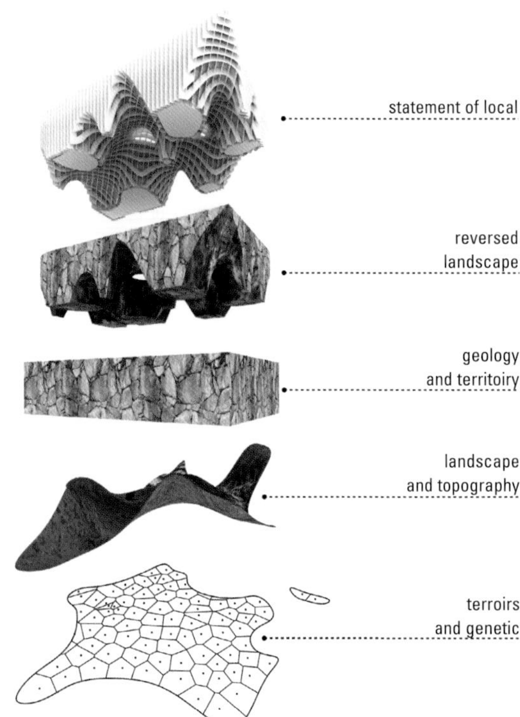

Diagram of the different layers that make up the internal space

View of the Pavilion from the Decumanus

View of internal space

51 **United Kingdom Pavilion Expo Milano 2015**

Wolfgang Buttress

The 1910 square metres of the United Kingdom Pavilion will develop around the concept of the hive, the role of bees and how new research and technologies are helping to address food safety and biodiversity. The humble bee plays a unique role in our ecosystem: between the culture and interactions in a bee colony and those in human societies, we can trace a strong parallel.

The pavilion consists of five main areas. Visitors to the United Kingdom Pavilion are greeted by an orchard; the second theme is the Meadow, 40-metres long; visitors cross a land corridor of Corten steel, open to the sky.

During the Expo period, the plants in the meadow will be changed continuously.

At the end of the meadow is an amphitheatre that provides an ideal resting place to discover the hive standing opposite.

The hive is a reticular 3-D structure, a 14 x 14 x 14 metre box in aluminium placed on columns of three meters in height. A spherical hollow dug into its interior allows visitors to go inside it. On the inside one has the sensation of being inside a real beehive, with the sounds and vibrations typical of bees.

Going back up to the top level, the visitor reaches the terrace.

This podium of 300 square metres, located above the architectural structure, has a large social space, including a bar. Situated beneath the terrace, the architectural structure, with the flexible auditorium that connects to a VIP area, provides a perfect space for conferences and events.

D.S.

View of the cloud/beehive in the centre of the pavilion

right
The meadow introducing to the central area of the beehive

52 Belgium Pavilion Expo Milano 2015

Patrick Genard y Asociados

Following Leon Battista Alberti's formula, "The house is a small city and the city a big house", the project aims to make the Belgian pavilion a reduced model of an excellent urban planning solution: the "Lobe City", which in this context becomes architecture. The residential neighbourhoods are the volumes-pavilions built in wood and the Farm draws on the light from the view of the surrounding greenery. The historic centre of the city becomes the atrium, the heart of the project, formalized by a large geodesic glass structure.

The pavilion's volumes are also allusions to Belgium's agricultural and horticultural architecture. The geodesic dome's large volume is a reference to the large Royal Greenhouses of Laeken, and the first volume, the Farm, reinterprets the traditional elongated shape of the Belgian farm with gabled roof, as well as the faceted wooden pavilions with organic contemporary shapes, this way bringing together the two eras.

The ramp inside the farm building takes us into an artificial basement, the Cave, where university projects and experiments on alternative food production will be exhibited, in response to the challenges and questions posed by Expo.

It will be a sustainable pavilion. Energy will be supplied by photovoltaic panels integrated into the glass roofs. The building will be equipped with effective insulation and will follow the direction of the sun allowing for control of natural light, while a cooling and water reuse strategy will allow for further energy savings.

The materials used for the pavilion's construction also represent Belgium.

Thus the Belgian pavilion is a perfect fit with the theme defined by the Expo 2015 organizers, creating a bridge between the traditional Belgian and Milan architectures, the Milanese architecture symbolized by Cascina Triulza.

D.S.

View of an exhibition space

Side view of the various elements of the pavilion

View of the Belgian Pavilion from the Decumanus

53 **Germany Pavilion Expo Milano 2015**

The working group ARGE of the German Pavilion Expo Milano 2015

The German Pavilion convincingly translates the German landscape of fields and meadows into an architectural language: a building designed as a slightly uphill scenic plateau, with a freely accessible surface and a thematic exhibition inside.

In this very recognizable meadow landscape stylized plants grow, "sprouting ideas" that rise from the exhibition to the surface, unfolding in a large canopy of leaves; this is the unifying element that connects the outer and inner spaces, the architecture and the exhibition.

With its open, free access plateau landscape, the German Pavilion does not qualify as an explicitly representational architecture, but rather as a place of meeting and exchange, and is therefore using the programmatic motto "Fields of Ideas".

The use of a variety of local timbers, with their different grains and colours, gives it a distinctive note, while the landscape of fields and meadows turns into a walkable wooden roof where wood is not only an empathic element but also a sign of a responsible use of raw reconstitutable materials characterized by a balance of CO2. The facade is formed by a horizontal lamellar structure that adapts itself to the facade, following the heights and various openings, with a reference to the horizontal layers of the soil.

The modern steel structure in membranes makes it extremely simple to build, thereby reducing the use of materials, while the unusual shapes which flow organically become a symbol of innovations that indicate the future modelled on nature.

D.S.

View of the German Pavilion from the Decumanus

View of the sails on the pavilion

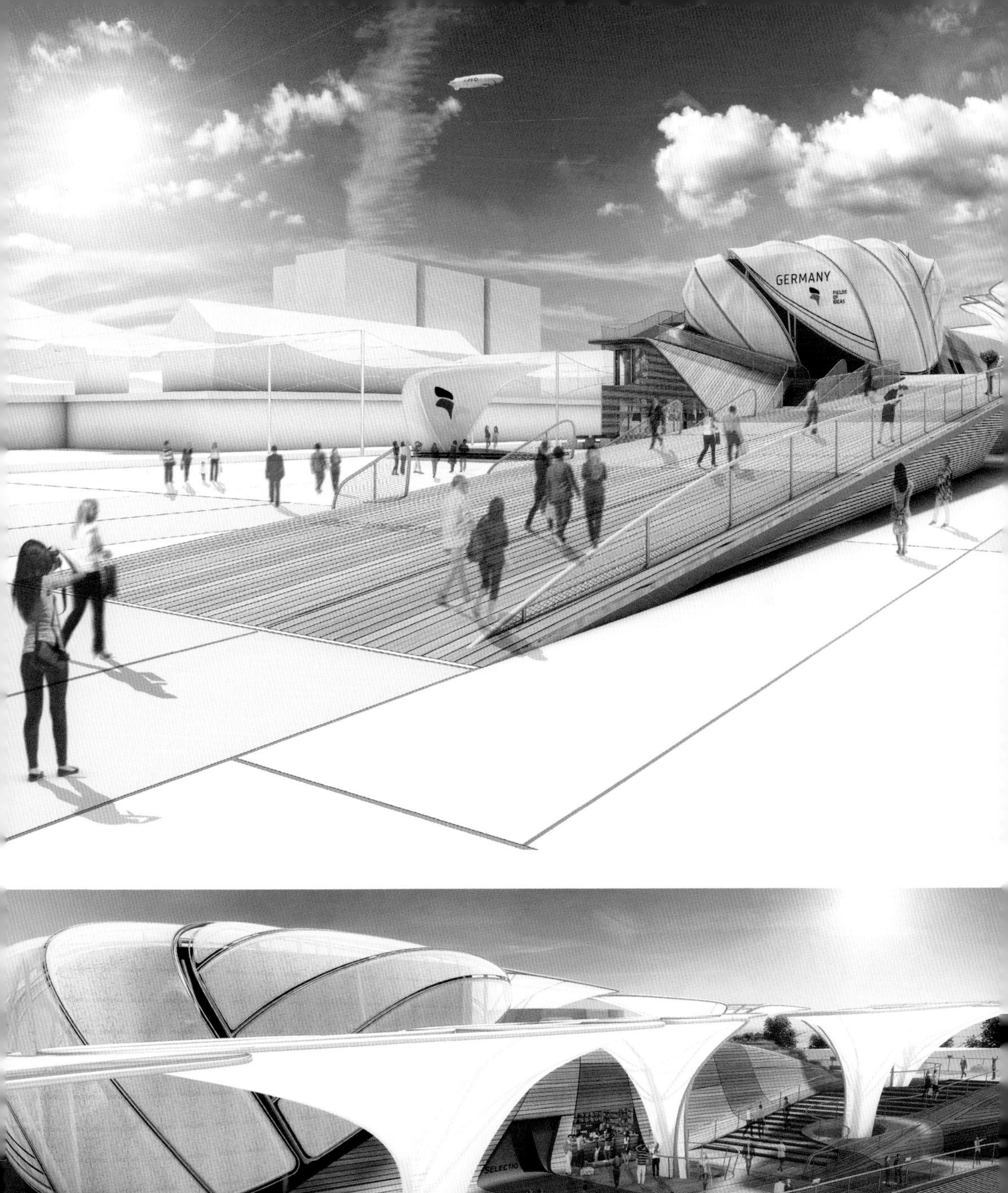
GERMANY
FIELDS
OF
IDEAS

54 Israel Pavilion Expo Milano 2015

Knafo Klimor Architects

The state of Israel is an extraordinary laboratory for studies in the field of agriculture: it exports its knowledge, experience and technology worldwide.

With the theme Fields of Tomorrow, the Israel Pavilion will demonstrate how Israel is a cutting edge country. The cultivation of rocky land, growing vegetables in the desert, the invention of new irrigation methods, and improving the quality of seeds, are all part of the birth of modern agriculture, marked by creativity and courage.

The main facade of the pavilion is a vertical field composed of modular tiles used for agricultural crops. In the field, large tiles are used to grow crops on a steel frame. Each tile contains a drip irrigation system, controlled by a computer, which ensures optimal cultivation and growth.

The field will consist of cereal varieties and other basic food products, and as a result, from a wide range of products that will deliver a mosaic of textures, smells and colours that change with the changing seasons.

The pavilion, for the most part, was built with advanced green technologies, including those for energy and water conservation and air treatment. The building is located at the centre of the park, in front of the Italian pavilion, adjacent to the Cardo and the Decumano roads, and visitors can stroll along its facade as part of the their experience.

Inside the pavilion, an exhibition will provide a virtual tour of Israel. The exhibition will present the technological innovations in agriculture that Israeli scientists are developing for the future.

The entire structure will be recycled at the end of the exposition. The Israeli pavilion in Milan 2015 presents a planning approach in which the architecture is a vehicle to promote sustainability, protection of natural resources and dedication to social prosperity for the future of humanity.

D.S.

Bird's eye view

View of the pavilion and the wall sections of living plants

55 Czech Republic Pavilion Expo Milano 2015

Chybik+Kristof Associated Architects

The Czech Republic pavilion at Expo 2015, located at the main entrance of the exhibition area, along the Decumano road, is surrounded by an urban pool. The building rises out of the water, is part of the water, and at the same time, the water itself is part of the pavilion.

The pavilion is made up of a modular building of 1,300 square metres. On the ground floor, there will be the shop and restaurant areas, on the first and second floors, exhibitions, while on the roof there will be a garden with over 350 square metres for the "Laboratory of Life". Built in just six weeks, the building was designed to be reused in the future, in accordance with the concepts of low environmental impact and sustainability.

Inside the pavilion space are four macro-areas.

The urban pool, located on the exterior, is a relaxation area where visitors can taste beer. The interior, however, is divided into three zones.

The first, called Country of Stories and Imagination, will recount the ancient and indissoluble link between the Czech cities and water, creating a "Bohemian" atmosphere for visitors.

The second area, accessible to visitors, is a veritable "laboratory of Life".

The third, called the Laboratory of Silence, is the heart of the pavilion as it hosts a complete example of a Bohemian forest habitat. The theme extends to the restaurant where traditional cuisine will be served.

Inside, therefore, the restaurants will give visitors the chance to experience the best of Bohemian cuisine, while the pool areas and the roof garden will be places where visitors can enjoy a relaxing break.

D.S.

The pool before the Pavilion is a free space for lounging

Aerial view of the pavilion with the pool in the foreground

56 Brazil Pavilion Expo Milano 2015

Studio Arthur Casas

The inspiration behind the Brazilian Pavilion is that of a flexible web or net, representing the diversity of the South American country. The Brazilian Pavilion proposes a pause; the intention is to create a piazza that brings together people and generates curiosity. The large structure is open to visitors and establishes a path between the various plant species grown in the country.

The colours of the steel structure are reminiscent of those in the Brazilian land and the gradual transition from the exterior to the interior aims at removing boundaries between architecture and scenic landscape. The metaphor of the web is symbolized by a tensile structure that creates unexpected places for leisure and relaxation. Following the tradition of Brazilian modernism and its pavilions, wide ramps reinforce the vertical connection between the various spaces.

The exhibition content, developed by the Atelier Marko Brajovic, places the focus on four main themes: Natural wisdom, the result of a millennial coexistence between man and an exuberant biodiversity; Empire of the colours, in the variety of Brazil's tropical plants and cultures; Human nutrition, the result of the sustainable use of natural resources and small-scale agriculture; Creative fusion, as the combination of high technology, productivity and responsible employment for a vast territory.

In the back of the pavilion is a structure that contains the exhibition space, an auditorium, a pop-up store, a cafeteria, a bar, a restaurant and the service office, all connected by a large atrium at the entrance that illuminates the pavilion with natural light. Brazilian designers and artists were invited to exhibit works that highlight Brazilian inventiveness, side by side with interactive installations that explain the technical revolution underway in the country's agricultural sector.

Sustainability is characterized by the construction system, made up of prefabricated modules, in the mechanisms for reusing rainwater and in the use of certified and recyclable materials.

Brazil wants to represent the possibility of new paradigms in development, capable of reconciling growth and conservation, diversity and originality, and openness and transformation.

D.S.

The colours of the structure recall the colours of nature in Brazil

The tensile net is fun, but is also a symbol because it leads visitors to discover the cultivation of selected varieties

57 USA Pavilion Expo Milano 2015

James Biber

The United States presents a dynamic pavilion that showcases America's unique role in the future of food throughout the world.

The USA Pavilion is made up of openings, transparency and accessibility, with sustainable design elements and a host of references to American culture.

The building itself is reminiscent of a barn with a perforated facade in red, white and blue aluminium on one side, and on the other side, a living wall as long as a football field.

On entering the hall, visitors are greeted by a series of images of specifically American food; a walkway made from wood from the Coney Island boardwalk rises from ground level to the second floor. Upstairs, there is a rooftop terrace that will host night-time parties and performances.

D.S.

View of the USA Pavilion from the Decumanus with its green facade

Internal space of the USA Pavilion

58 **Japan Pavilion Expo Milano 2015**

Atsushi Kitagawara Architects, Ishimoto Architectural & Engineering Firm, Inc., Arup, IPARCH, Stain Engineering

The Japan Pavilion draws inspiration for its theme, Harmonious diversity, from the traditional processes of diversification and reversibility of the various Japanese productions and industries, aimed at principles that are in harmony with nature and the enhancement of renewable resources to preserve the ecosystem. The sphere of nutrition, the main theme of EXPO 2015, refers to the same criteria; the richness of Japanese cuisine is an integral part of this balance, both for its culinary variety and for the artisan production related to the field. The symbol chosen for the pavilion is therefore the traditional chopsticks that reveal the Japanese philosophy of food, as it relates to such values as gratitude, moderation and sharing.

The pavilion has an impressive exterior entrance ramp, a long terraced serpentine walkway that serves as a roof for the exhibition rooms beneath it, leading to the upper floor of the main volume. It is made up of a series of linear spaces, arranged in ascending order of size, up to the largest complex on two floors, including the ground floor reserved for the exhibition, and the first floor for catering and events. From the outside, the structure appears as a dense three-dimensional self-supporting grid made of Japanese larch, a very deep honeycomb lattice that covers the building and gives the lively effect of light and shade along the facades. The use of a renewable resource like wood for the construction of the pavilion also reflects the desire to emphasize the concept of sustainability, the importance of the relationship between man and the environment through the tree's emblematic role in nature and in Japanese culture.

Thanks to the innovative use of wood, the project is a successful synthesis between the Japanese building tradition, with a special reference to the tongue and groove joint techniques used in the temples, and the new technologies for analysis and modelling.
M.T.

Aerial view of the Japanese Pavilion

The external structure with three-dimensional self-supporting lattice grid in Japanese larch wood

59

Mexico Pavilion Expo Milano 2015

Francisco López Guerra Almada

Corn is native to Mexico and indeed man's origins are attributed to it. The concept for the Mexican Pavilion arose from this deep relationship, a tribute and a homage to a product of the earth which for Mexicans is a daily source of life.

Therefore, the outer membrane of the façade is inspired by corn cobs. The membrane lets in daylight, and by night becomes a warmly coloured light. The Pavilion's architecture, deeply symbolic, is designed to give visitors a sensory experience. The interiors reflect the local agricultural systems during the time of King Nezahualcóyotl (about 1400), when the rainwater was collected and channelled into terraces at high altitudes and made to drain downwards towards the valleys to irrigate large areas of farmland. Therefore, inside the pavilion the visitor will find ramps, podiums and terraces that create different museological areas. The water gushes from the top, falling down through the center to create a lush internal garden.

The intention behind the botanical garden is to give the visitor contact with the great diversity of Mexican flora, to recount the sustainability and the wealth of the typical products in the local cuisine. The spiral ramps allow visitors to move from the access piazza to the various exhibition levels and ensures constant and dynamic flows.

The aim of the Mexican Pavilion is to give a picture of the entire culture, starting with the ancestors and arriving at the current scientific and technological research: it is a place to learn about the country's deeply rooted traditions and its innovations.
A.M.

Longitudinal section

External view with corncob inspired roof

Internal exhibition space

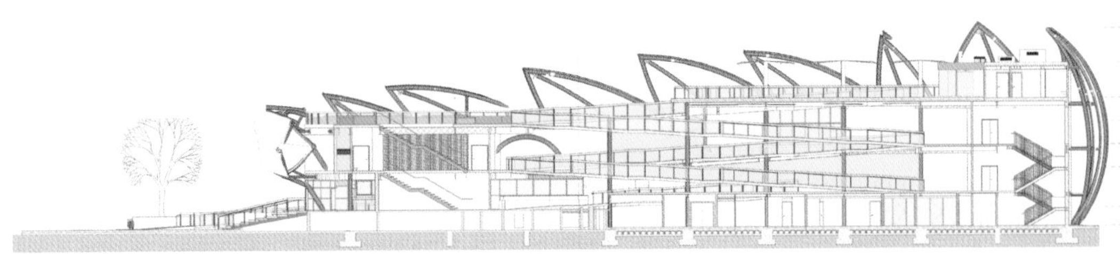

60 **Chile Pavilion**
Chile Pavilion Expo Milano 2015

Cristián Undurraga

The Chile Pavilion has the look of a ship's deck in laminated wood, and it is this latticework skeleton on which the building's expression and formal synthesis rely. Its regular volume rests on six steel pillars, each composed of three arms. This strategy frees up the ground floor, providing a visual transparency and free movement of the public, as well as establishing a close relationship between the urban space and the open space of the pavilion, transforming the boundary between public and private into a common border.

From a distance, the building appears as one whole (on a monumental scale), while close-up one sees the fragmented quality in wood, which interacts with the body and gives it a human scale.

The pine wood with which the pavilion was built was imported from Chile, while the laminating process was done in Italy.

The regular quality of the upper "casing" and the neutral nature of the interior space provide the flexibility necessary for exhibitions and accommodating the different audio-visual equipment. The neutral nature of the pavilion is part of a strategy to reuse it, and after Expo, it will be transported to Chile.
D.S.

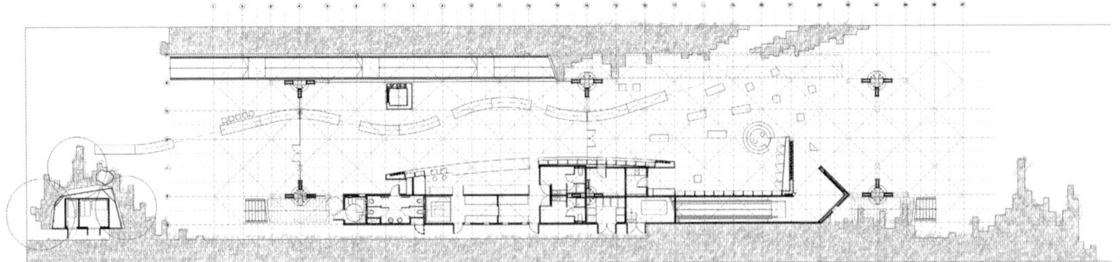

Ground floor layout

External view of the monumental wooden construction

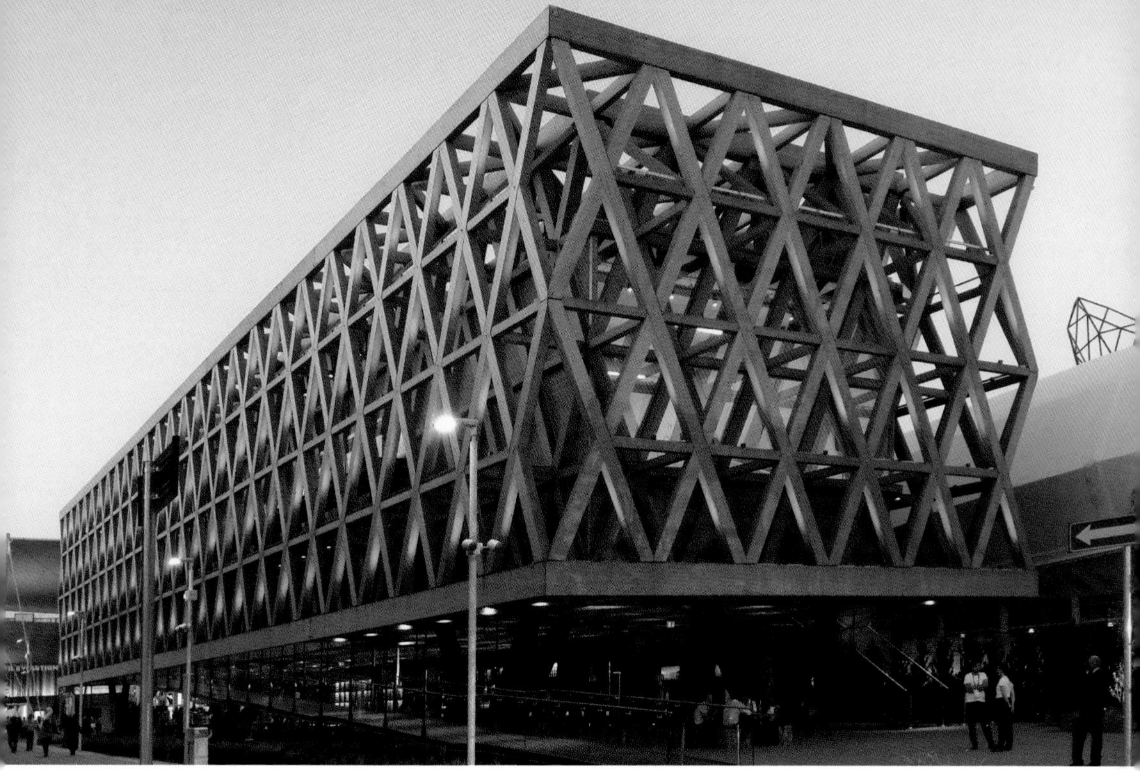

61 **China Pavilion Expo Milano 2015**

Tsinghua University & Studio Link-Arc

The China Pavilion is designed as a field of spaces, like a cloud hovering over a "land of hope." The design concept for the Pavilion is a series of public programs situated under a floating roof, a stunningly designed structure with great symbolic value. The theme for the China Pavilion is "The Land of Hope", a concept embodied by the undulating shape of the roof, the result of a fusion between the outline of a city skyline on the north side of the building and that of a natural landscape on south side: this fusion expresses the idea of a "hope" that can become reality when a city and nature harmoniously coexist.

Conceived as a wooden structure that uses the "Beam" system as a point of reference, a traditional Chinese architectural element, the pavilion roof also employs modern technology to create long spans that are suited to the public nature of the building. The roof is covered with panels of tiles, in reference to the construction of the traditional ceramic roof, but they are reinterpreted as large bamboo leaves that soften the outline of the roof that shades the public spaces below.

Under this great covering, we find a landscape where wheat is grown on the ground floor, a reference to China's agricultural past.

This natural landscape creates a seamless transition from an agricultural system to a multimedia LED system in the centre of the pavilion, the centrepiece of the building's exhibition program. There are numerous exhibition and cultural spaces in the pavilion, arranged in sequence, starting from the outside area that leads the visitor to the inside through multimedia installations, exhibitions, and short films about Chinese culture. At the end of the tour is a large terrace located above the bamboo roof with an extensive view of the Expo park.

D.S.

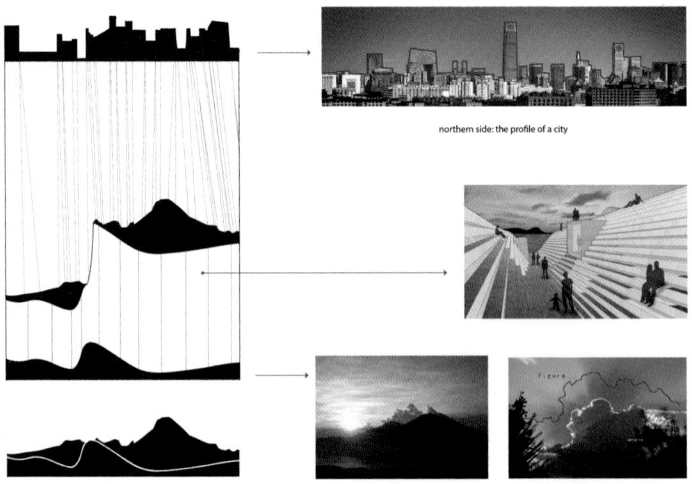

northern side: the profile of a city

southern side: the profile of a landscape

Preparatory sketch of original project

External view of the pavilion, green-planted area in the foreground

Aerial view of the Chinese Pavilion

62 **Colombia Pavilion**
Expo Milano 2015

Mauricio Cardenas Laverde

The design for the Colombia Pavilion has interpreted the Expo theme by dividing the building into five different levels of elevation and climate, namely: Caribbean 0.00 metres a.s.l., Amazon and Orinoco 1,000 metres a.s.l., Coffee-growing and industrial zone 1,000–2,000 metres a.s.l., the Andes 2,000–3,000 metres a.s.l., Paramo and Glaciers 3,000–4,000 metres a.s.l. and above, all of which represent the different thermal floors.

In this way the Columbia Pavilion is both a kind of representation of the area of natural resources, and an epistemological map of music, cuisine, industry and the historical and cultural heritage.

From the functional point of view the building is as follows: the first floor of every module up to module four is dedicated to the visitor's route. At module 4 the visitor descends to a screening in the auditorium on the ground floor. On the ground floor, visitors will still have free access to the coffee shop, the Sponsor Exhibition, the restaurant and shop. The main concept behind the facade is that of "walking through". The facade is in fact composed of vertical slats that on the three sides have three different graphic displays illustrating Columbia and its thermal levels. As the visitor moves through the building, they can see the different designs and experience the changing perception of them, as happens during a trip along the pisos termicos. This way the observer directly becomes the architect of the façade's dynamism, the façade becoming a communication tool in which images and messages are explored, based on the movement of people going through it. The facade is therefore an ever-changing element, as are the climates, the landscapes, the culture and the products of Colombia as one walks through its climate zones.

The pavilion is entirely "dry" built. The laminated wood structure can be easily assembled and dismounted, and since the size of the individual pieces allows for its transport in containers and other means of transportation, the individual pieces completed at Expo can be moved and reused. The dynamic facade was also designed as an instrument through which the visitor moves through space: the result is a low tech and sustainable surface.
D.S.

The four volumes of the pavilion represent the four climactic zones of Colombia

left
In the evening the dynamic exterior comes to life inviting visitors to move in space

63 **Kuwait Pavilion Expo Milano 2015**

Italo Rota

The challenge of nature is Kuwait's central theme, and its pavilion is dedicated to three major themes such as water, agriculture and energy.

The Pavilion, designed by Italo Rota, has the profile of the dhow, the traditional boats that sail the Gulf. The exhibition is divided into three sections: the traditional landscape of Kuwait, the scientific research developed to transform it, and the encounter with the cuisine, hospitality and the products of this country.

The entrance to the Pavilion, made entirely of steel frame, is distinguished by large sails that invite the visitor to enter, while the side walls of the complex, 2,970 square metres in size, are distinguished by a large greenhouse for the hydroponic production of plants, which will then be eaten in the restaurant at the back. *D.S.*

View of the pavilion entrance from the Decumanus

View of the huge sails that make up the pavilion

One of the internal exhibition spaces

64 Slow Food Pavilion Expo Milano 2015

Herzog & de Meuron

From the very beginning of the planning stage, the Expo 2015 Slow Food pavilion designed by the Swiss firm Herzog & de Meuron, was able to rely on the collaboration of Carlo Petrini, founder of the Slow Food Association that inspired the name of the pavilion.

The building is located in a special area of the Expo master plan, a triangular space at the eastern end of the Decumanus that is certainly destined to become one of the main public discussion forums.

The architectural and exhibition pavilion concept is based on a simple layout: it is composed of three long narrow buildings that recall the cascina, the traditional Lombardy agricultural farm building.

The three buildings are dedicated to exhibition display, food tasting, and to social gatherings and are arranged to create an internal triangular space for use as a courtyard or marketplace.

The pavilion is designed to help visitors discover the importance of agricultural and food biodiversity, to explore the wide range of products in this category and to become aware of the need to adopt new consumer habits.

Visitors will be able to learn about biodiversity through audio-visual presentations, and through reading key texts concerning our consumer habits and their impact on the planet. They will be able to meet and talk to sustainable agricultural and local food growing representatives, to gain deeper insight into agricultural and food biodiversity. After the Expo Fair, in keeping with the Slow Food initiative entitled "Orto in condotta", a national scholastic program aimed at food and environmental education, the pavilions will be dismantled and reassembled as garden sheds in vegetable gardens in schools throughout Italy.

G.P.

Pavilion layout

View of the centre piazza surrounded by three buildings

Internal view of the pavilion

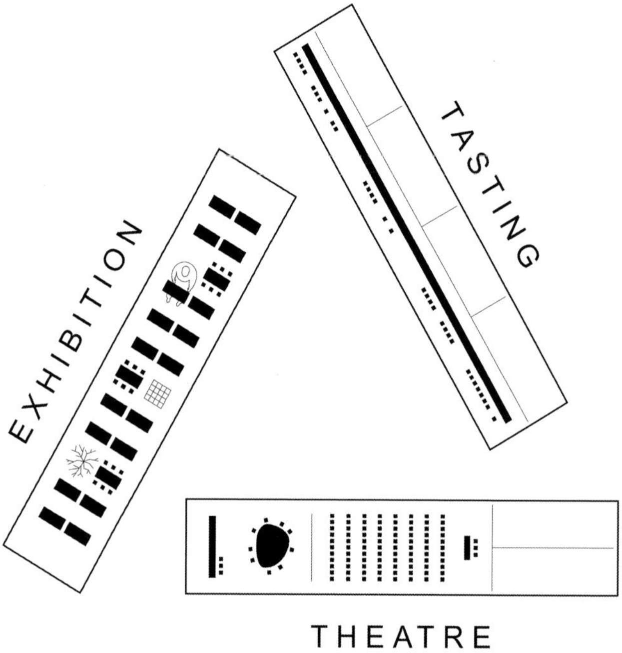

EXHIBITION

TASTING

THEATRE

Discover
Biodiversity
Taste
Biodiversity

Slow Food Theater

65 Intesa Sanpaolo Pavilion Expo Milano 2015

Michele De Lucchi

The pavilion that Michele De Lucchi has designed for Intesa Sanpaolo at Expo 2015 is located near the intersection of the Cardo and Decumano avenues, the main thoroughfares. It has a strong personality and focusses on environmental impact, representing the bank in its actions, and promoting the commitment to sustainable development.

The natural shape of the Pavilion is a result of reflection on the world, sustainability, the unstoppable flow of time and the impossibility of programming or battling against natural events. The architectural concept recalls the shape of three stones worn smooth by water, and the architect De Lucchi drew his inspiration from a Hindu story. The story tells us that "to gain wisdom and happiness, we must become like the stones in the river, stones that know that the water will always inevitably pass over them. The stone lets it go past and lets the current slide around its skin, smoothing the roughness, modelling the body."

The Pavilion is located on a body of water, which has smoothed its shape, digging a furrow into the facade.

The outer cover is made with white shingles that create a unique pattern, reminiscent of the rooftops on mountain buildings; a second skin protects the wood from the elements; the empty cavity between the two walls acts as thermal insulation. On the inside, the structure is made entirely of exposed and laminated wood, recalling rural buildings; the floors are made of oak, outdoor spaces are covered with grass and the paths are made of Greenwood, wood dust from waste materials.

The Pavilion has two floors. On the ground floor, there is an operational subsidiary branch of Intesa Sanpaolo and a convertible exhibition space, enriched by a multimedia installation by Studio Azzurro that represents the bank's values and its focus on culture, the territory and the heritage of Italian identity. Upstairs, the foyer welcomes the guests who will be going to the VIP Lounge, dedicated to private business meetings.

Within the Expo theme — "Feeding the Planet, Energy for Life" — which calls for a conscious and responsible development for the future of the planet, the Intesa Sanpaolo pavilion takes great care in addressing the issues of sustainability and the environment.
V.M.

Internal view of one of the first floor spaces

The Intesa Sanpaolo Pavilion overlooks a reflection pool

Preparatory sketch by Michele De Lucchi

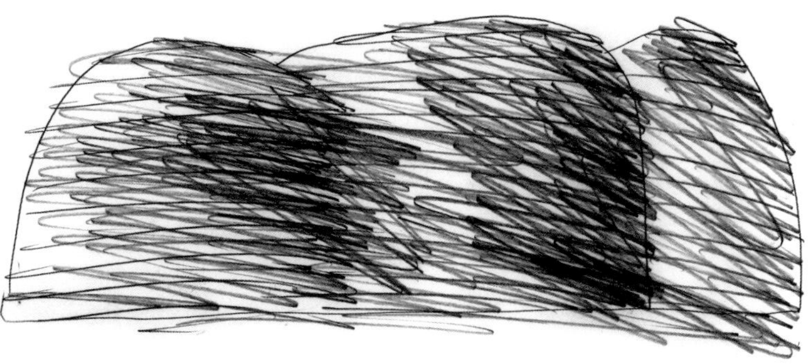

66 **Piacenza Pavilion Expo Milano 2015**

eartHand Project

The eartHand project grew from the desire to represent Piacenza and its territorial identity in its various specific aspects: from its historical and cultural heritage and landscape to its wine making and gastronomic excellence, from the great innovations in science and technology to the people who made this territory what it already was historically, and is today, an important crossroads of history, culture and peoples.

The Earth is the element and the concept that sums up the true significance of the land of Piacenza, understood in its various meanings: production of raw material, transformation by man, wealth from the various processes, historical sedimentation and stratification.

The name eartHand declares the will to perpetually bind together two factors: earth, the primitive and generating material element; and hand, the symbol of man and his energy and ability to shape the earth.

eartHand is presented as the great metaphor of the essence of Piacenza: a clod of earth extracted from the ground, raised into the air and transformed into an icon for transport to Milan Expo 2015. Externally, a dense material mass, compact and stratified like a fortress, while the interior becomes a surface to explore, narrating the complexity and richness of the region's values, like an archaeological excavation.

The "clod" pavilion is a square prism with a base of 6 metres on each side and 7 metres in height. The pavilion interior has been left empty to provide the maximum display space, with an uneven faceted surface, a complex system of cavities that are partially interactive, some parts vacant, some parts transparent to accommodate video projection systems, others opaque to become surfaces on which to project images, culminating at the top in a wide octagonally shaped opening, recalling one of the distinctive architectures of Piacenza, the octagonal tower of Sant'Antonino.

The construction system, made with prefabricated modules and mounted during construction, is composed of a steel cantilever structure supported by columns, also in steel, integrated into the rear section. A system of metal frames is attached directly to the primary structure to support the weight of the panels that complete the enclosure.

Almost in contrast to the external treatment of the front facades, the inner finishing of the central kaleidoscope is composed of smooth luminous interactive technological panels.
C.G.

External view of the compact stratified "clod" of earth

Internal view of the octagonal Piacenza Pavilion tower

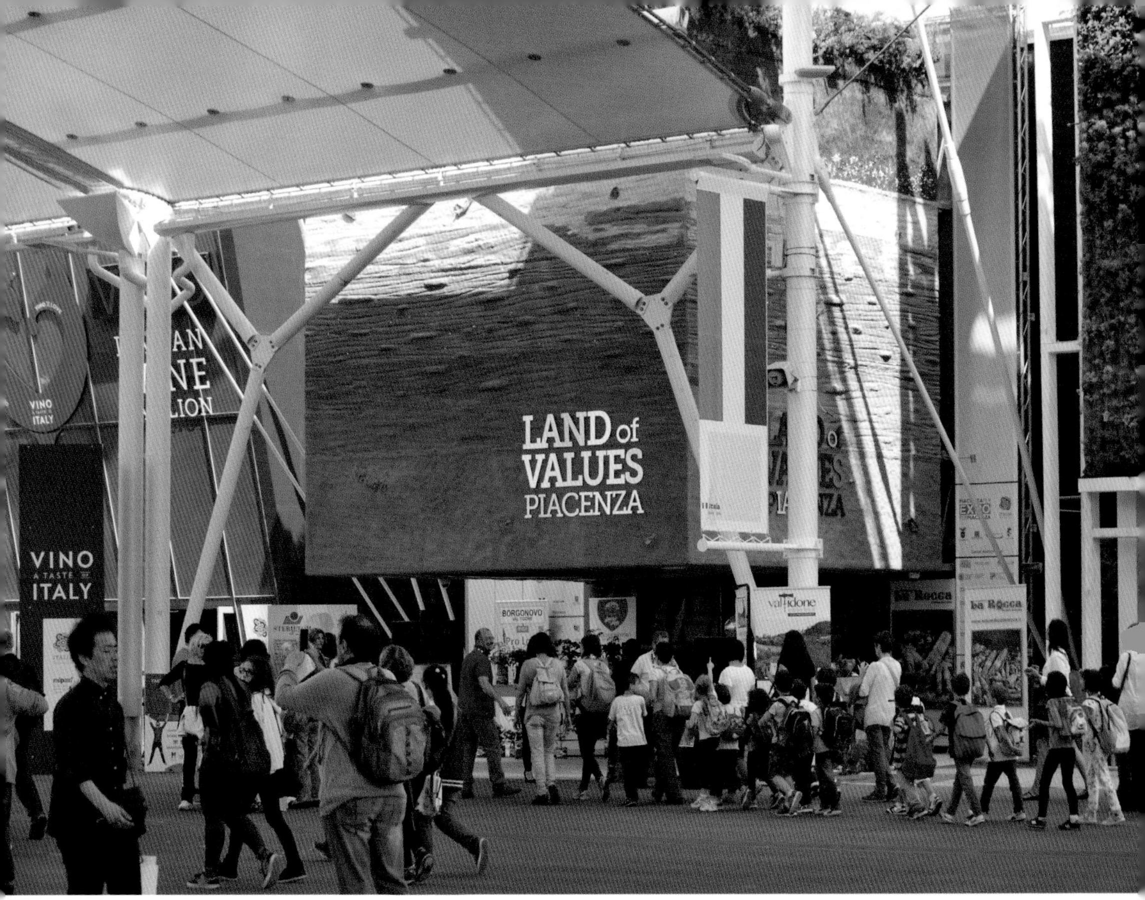
LAND of
VALUES
PIACENZA
VINO
A TASTE OF
ITALY
BORGONOVO
valtidone
La Rocca

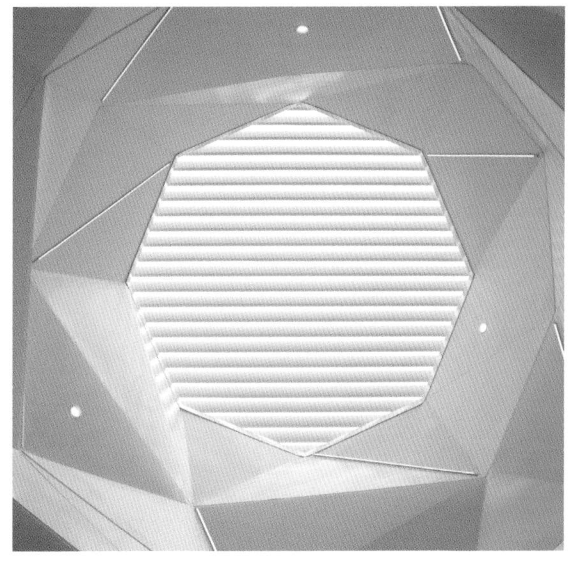

Credits

Milan Centre

Expo Gate
Via Luca Beltrami
Client
La Triennale di Milano Servizi s.r.l., Expo 2015 S.p.A.
Architectural project
Alessandro Scandurra – Scandurra Studio Architettura
Project team
Alessandro Scandurra, Nicola Bianchi, Davide Sala, Giovanni Nardin, Poé Matteo George
Structural project design
Redesco s.r.l.
Systems installation project
Coprat soc.coop.
Contractor
ICG s.r.l, Stahlbau Pichler s.r.l., Fantin S.p.A., IMG s.r.l.
Photography
Filippo Romano

Atelier Castello
Piazza Castello
Architectural project design
Guidarini & Salvadeo + Snark space making
Team
Stefano Guidarini, Pierluigi Salvadeo, Marco Lampugnani Yulya Besplemennova, Camilla Ceschi, Camilla Marini, Martina Pini, Marco Pioventini, Riccardo Spreafico, Luca Varvello, Chiara Bianchi, Lucalberto Bordignon, Marta Iole Procaccio, Clara Michielon, Moreno Marrazzo
Photography
Guidarini&Salvadeo+Snark

Triennale Terrace Restaurant
Viale Alemagna
Designers
OBR Paolo Brescia and Tommaso Principi
Consultants
Buro Happold Engineering
Milan Ingegneria
DBA Progetti
GAD Studio Global
Assistance Development
Maddalena D'Alfonso
Antonio Perazzi Studio del Paesaggio
Rossi Bianchi Lighting Design
Artiva Design
Suono e Vita – Acoustic engineering
Marzia Bianchi
Collaborating contractors
Andrea Casetto, Elisa Siffredi, Maria Lezhnina, Teresa Corbin, Enrico Pinto, Cecilia Pastore, Giulia Negri
Customer
Triennale di Milano
Photography
Michele Nastasi

Litta residential building
Corso Magenta, via Illica
aMDL architect Michele De Lucchi, chief architect Giovanna Latis
Client
Valcomp Tre S.p.A.
Architectural project design and artistic direction
Michele De Lucchi
Project manager
Giovanna Latis
Project team
Agnieszka Burdajewicz, Matteo Del Marco, Alessandra De Leonardis, Sang Yeun Lee, Filippo Meda
Models
Francesco Faccin, Giuseppe Filippini, Francesco Codicè
Graphics
Davide Angeli, Rossella Piccaluga, Alessia Tosini
Asset Management
Anselmo Comito, Luca Percassi
Consultants:
Mechanical and electrical systems
Fire department alarm acoustics
Hilson Moran Italia
Structural project design
Comes s.r.l.
Parking consultants
MIC
Network and underground services
Alpina S.p.A.
Worksite safety calculations and coordination
P&M s.r.l.
Green spaces
Franco Giorgetta Landscape architect
Construction
Impresa Percassi F.lli s.r.l.
Archeosystems
Gasparoli Restoration and maintenance
Capoferri Doors and windows
Site Manager
Dario Menini
Time span
2008-2014
Photography
Marco Beck Peccoz

Priceless Restaurant Milan
Piazza della Scala
Project
MasterCard Europe. With the participation of Intesa San Paolo
Event
4Ward, Milano
Architectural project and design
Park Associati, Milano
Contractor
Fourproject, Paderno Dugnano
Lighting
Flos Lighting, Milano
Internal seating
Driade, Milano
External seating
Saporiti Italia
Electrical appliances
Electrolux-Zanussi
Flooring
Mirage Granito Ceramico, Pavullo (Mo)
Photography
Andrea Martiradonna

Redevelopment of the Ospedale Maggiore Policlinico, Mangiagalli and Regina Elena area
Via Francesco Sforza
Central Building and Sforza Tower
Client, promoter
Fondazione IRCCS Ca' Granda Ospedale Maggiore Policlinico
Intervention area
80,000 square metres
Constructed surface area
70,000 square metres
2007 International competition - 1° prize: Boeri Studio (S. Boeri, G. Barreca, G. La Varra) in ATI with Techint S.p.A., ABDarchitetti, B.T.C. srl, C+S Architects, Labics, Land s.r.l., TRT Trasporti e Territorio s.r.l.)
2009/2010 Preliminary project, final project and artistic direction: Barreca & La Varra, Stefano Boeri Architetti collaborating contractors: F. Cesa Bianchi (coordination), S. Gangemi, A. Grassi, F. Lampis, M. Ranieri, A. Sfikas
Client
Fondazione IRCCS Ca' Granda Ospedale Maggiore Policlinico
International competition - 1°prize (2007): Boeri Studio (Stefano Boeri, Gianandrea Barreca, Giovanni La Varra) in ATI with Techint SpA, ABDA architetti, B.T.C. srl, C+S Architects, Labics, Land srl, TRT Trasporti e Territorio srl
Preliminary project, final

project and artistic direction: Barreca & La Varra, Stefano Boeri Architetti
Intervention area
80,000 square metres
Constructed surface area
70,000 square metres
Time span
2007 –ongoing construction
www.barrecaelavarra.it
www.stefanoboeriarchitetti.net
www.policlinico.mi.it
Mortuary and logistics department of new Ospedale Policlinico di Milano
Project
ABDArchitetti botticini – de appolonia & associati, C+S Architects
www.botticini-arch.com
www.deappolonia-arch.com
web.cipiuesse.it
Collaborating contractors
A. Alberti, A. Guarneri, D. Ledo
Client
Fondazione Ospedale Maggiore Policlinico, Mangiagalli and Regina Elena di Milano
Structural project
Studio Ingegneria Lazzari
Consultants during project stage
Techint S.p.A.
Technical systems
Techint S.p.A.

Redevelopment of the Complesso Balneare Caimi Via Carlo Botta
Giovanna Latis, Elena Martucci, Laboratorio permanente - Nicola Russi, Angelica Sylos Labini and artistic direction by Michele De Lucchi and Andrée Ruth Shammah
Client
Fondazione Pier Lombardo
General project artistic direction
Andrée Ruth Shammah and Michele De Lucchi
Construction company
Ricci SpA
Site manager
Ing. Valerio Arienti
Fire prevention project
Gae Engineering Srl - ing. Giuseppe Amaro, with Daniela Amato
Redevelopment of the swimming pool and external areas
Architectural project
Giovanna Latis, Elena Martucci, Nicola Russi
with the collaboration of
Angelica Sylos Labini, Luca De Stasio, Pietro Ferrario, Mario Ventilato, Giulia Spagnolo, Filippo Meda, Nicola Boccadoro, Neri D'Alessandro, Vincenzo Vella
Plumbing, mechanical and electrical systems
Beta Progetti - ing. Luigi Berti
Multifunctional sunken space
Architectural project design
Giovanna Latis
with the collaboration of
Nicola Boccadoro
Structural project design
Ing. Pietro Boerio
Mechanical and electrical systems
Beta Progetti - ing. Luigi Berti
Palazzina (Small building)
Architectural project design
Laboratorio permanente - Nicola Russi, Angelica Sylos Labini
With the collaboration of
Luca De Stasio, Pietro Ferrario, Mario Ventilato, Giulia Spagnolo, Evgeniya Dubova
Structural project design
Ing. Pietro Boerio
Mechanical systems
Studio Tecnico Ingegneria Impiantistica - P.I. Termotecnico Pierluigi Gandolfi
Electrical systems
Studio Corti - for Ind Alessandro Corti
Changing rooms
Architectural project design
Elena Martucci
With consulting service by Vincenzo Vella and collaboration of Giuseppe Riera and Ivan Zazzali
Structural project design
Eng. Pietro Boerio
Technical systems
Ricci SpA, Beta Progetti

Apartment building Viale Monte Grappa 16
Project
Westway Architects, Luca Aureggi, Maurizio Condoluci
www.westway.it
Client
Monte Grappa S.r.l.
Site manager and Structural project design
Progetti & Strutture
Construction company
Italiana Costruzioni S.p.A., Roma
Consultants during project stage
Conteco (energy certification and quality control), Ai Group (Technical installation Project)
Photography
Moreno Maggi

Hotel Duca D'Aosta Piazza Duca d'Aosta
Project
Onsitestudio
Client
Reale Immobili S.p.a.
Time span
2012 (competition) - 2015
Project Team
Competition stage
Angelo Lunati, Giancarlo Floridi with Chiara Molinari, Andrea Morstabilini, Luca Penucchini, with Giulia Pagliara, Orianne Scourzic, Federico Rosson
Project stage
Angelo Lunati, Giancarlo Floridi with Tommaso Brambati, Michele Miserotti, Chiara Molinari, Andrea Morstabilini, with Federico Bettazzi, Christina Tsompanoglou, Sebastian Sanchez, Samuel Silva, Maja Tanevska
Project work coordination
Starching
Structural project design
Redesco Progetti S.r.l.
Electrical systems
Europrogetti Engineering S.r.l.
Mechanical systems
Studio Massacesi S.r.l.
Fire protection project
AFC S.r.l.
Test inspector
Eng. Gabriele Cozzaglio

Excelsior Hotel Gallia Piazza Duca d'Aosta
Project
Studio Marco Piva
Client
Katara Hospitality
Project
Luxury 5 star Hotel
235 rooms : 188 standard rooms + 45 suites
One Presidential Suite, one Royal Suite
Assignment
Studio Marco PivaArchitettura, Landscape, Lighting, Interior Design
Site area
4,273 square metres
Constructed surface area
30,840 gross square metres

Porta Nuova Garibaldi
Pelli Clarke Pelli Architects, Muñoz + Albin, CZA Cino Zucchi Architetti, Studio Land, Piuarch
Masterplan Porta Nuova Garibaldi
Project
Pelli Clarke Pelli Architects (Cesar Pelli, Fred W. Clarke, Rafael Pelli)
Client
Hines Italia SGR S.p.a.
www.pcparch.com
www.porta-nuova.com
Porta Nuova Garibaldi – Offices and Retail space
Category
Offices, retail space
A,B, and C towers
Project
Pelli Clarke Pelli Architects (Cesar Pelli, Fred W. Clarke, Rafael Pelli)
Client
Hines Italia SGR S.p.a.
Time span
2006, 2012
www. pcparch.com
E1E2 Building
Project
Piuarch
Client
Hines Italia SGR S.p.a.
Time span
2006, 2013
Competition by invitation, prize winner
Architectural project design
Piuarch - Francesco Fresa, Germán Fuenmayor, Gino Garbellini, Monica Tricario
www.piuarch.it
Esecutive architectural project design
Tekne S.p.a.
Structural project design
MSC Associati S.r.l.
Technical systems
Ariatta Ingegneria dei Sistemi S.r.l.
Landscaping project
Land S.r.l.
Construction company
Colombo Costruzioni Spa
Site manager
Ing. G. Ceruti
Piuarch team
Gianni Mollo, Yusuke Aizawa, Erica Cazzaniga, Marco Dragoni, Yuji Kobayashi, Andres Mahdjoubian, Hirotaka Oishi, Antonio Pisanò, Claudia Savastano, Salvatore Seggio
Supplier companies
STO Italia, Sipam, Basf, NExus, IGuzzini, Ciapponi Gianfranco, Model System Italia
Photography
Andrea Martiradonna
Porta Nuova Garibaldi - Landscaping

Project
LAND Milano S.r.l.
www.landsrl.com
Designer
Andreas Kipar
LAND Group team
Adriana Pinate, Cecilia Pirani, Valerio Bozzoli Parasacchi, Giuliano Garello, Gianluca Lugli, Sonia Mastropietro, Valeria Pagliaro, Nicola Canepa, Sandra Paola Herrera, Ivan Maestri, Maria Vittoria Mastella, Michal Rucinski, Ilaria Sangaletti
Client
Hines Italia SGR S.p.a.
Le Residenze di Corso Como (Residential complex)
Project
Muñoz + Albin with Tekne (local partner), Coima Image
Client
Hines Italia SGR S.p.A.
Residential: 50 units - 5 storeys
Commercial: 12 units
www.munozalbin.com
La Corte Verde residential building in Corso Como
Project
Cino Zucchi Architetti
Client
Hines Italia SGR S.p.A.
Developer
Hines Italia srl
Investors
Istituto nazionale di previdenza dei Giornalisti italiani "Giovanni Amendola"
Slp
4,026 square metres
Construction period
February 2011 - June 2013
Architectural project design
Cino Zucchi Architetti - Cino Zucchi, Andrea Viganò, Sarah Zezza, Enrica Mannelli, Chiara Molinari, Chiara Toscani con Laura Mio
Graphics
Diego Martinelli
Model
One Off with Stefano Goffi
Rendering
Struttura Leggera with Matteo Vecchi and Filippo Zampese
Artistic direction
Cino Zucchi Architetti - Cino Zucchi, Andrea Viganò, Sarah Zezza
Structural design
Studio Ingegneria Lazzari
Mechanical systems
Tekser S.r.l.
Electrical systems
Tekser S.r.l.
Fire prevention project
FVR Engineering
Cost evaluation
Studio Luraschi – J&A Consultants
Interior design
Dolce Vita Homes in collaboration with Coima Image
Project and construction management
Hines srl - Coima srl
Photography
Filippo Poli

UniCredit Pavilion Porta Nuova
Project
Michele De Lucchi
Internal surface
3,300 square metres
Client
UniCredit Business Integrated Solutions Scpa
Project management
Hines Italia S.r.l
Construction management
COIMA S.r.l
Architectural project design
Architetto Michele De Lucchi S.r.l. – Michele De Lucchi
Project Manager
Arch. Nicholas Bewick
Project team
Arch. Francesco Garofoli, arch. Vittorio Romano, arch. Giorgio Traverso
Graphic design
Maddalena Molteni
Rendering
Moreno Marrazzo, arch. Marcello Biffi
Structural project design
MSC Associati S.r.l.
Technical systems
Ariatta Ingegneria dei Sistemi S.r.l.
Consultants:
Facade project design
Eurodesign S.a.s. di Adriano Crotti & C.
Fire prevention and safety projects
GTP S.r.l. l
Technical lighting project
Gruppo C14 S.r.l.
Acoustics and AV project
Studio di Ingegneria Acustica Marcello Brugola
Test technicians
J&A Consultants S.r.l.
Building practice consultants
Tekne S.p.a.
LEED Consultants
Greenwich S.r.l.
Site photography
Gabriella Nocera and Gianni Penzo - UniCredit

E3_East Office Building Porta Nuova
Project
MCA Mario Cucinella Architects
Time span
2013 – ongoing construction
Category
Design competition by invitation –equal first prize winner with studio Michele de Lucchi
Client
Hines Italia SGR S.p.A.
Surface
2,060 square metres
Project: Mario Cucinella Architects
Team: Mario Cucinella, Riccardo Minghini (Project Manager), Alberto Menozzi, Enrico Pintabona, Luca Stramigioli, Yuri Costantini (modellist) for preliminary and final stages; Luca Sandri, Alberto Casarotto, Marco Dell'Agli, Alberto Bruno, Giuseppe Perrone for concept stage
Rendering
Gruppo C14

Porta Nuova Varesine
Arquitectonica, Caputo Partnership, Antonio Citterio Patricia Viel and Partners, Coima Image, Dolce Vita Homes, Kohn Pedersen Fox Associates, LAND, Studio M2P Associati
Photographers
Marco Introini, Marco Garofalo © 2012 - Stefano Gusmeroli © 2012
Solaria and Aria buildings
Project
Arquitectonica
Client
Hines Italia SGR on behalf of Fondo Porta Nuova Varesine
Area
22,300 square metres
www.arquitectonica.com
Solea
Project
Paolo Caputo - Caputo Partnership
www.caputopartnership.it
Urban project team
Luciana De Rossi, Silvia Cingano, Simona Cornegliani
Architectural project and artistic direction team
Simona Cornegliani, Petra Hirsch, Alessandro Finozzi, Fabrizio Ruiu
Internal projects
Alida Forte Catella - COIMA Image with Dolce Vita Home
Structural project
Arup Italia S.p.A.
Technical systems
Deerns Italia
Main contractor
CMB Unieco
Construction company
Covar società consortile
Facades
CNS
Internal/external doors and windows
CNS external doors and windows - Lualdi internal doors
Staging and décor for entrance foyer and upper floor lobbies
Monti di Rovello – Boiseries: Entrance foyer and lobbies, Paolo Castelli – counters, Oikos – reinforced gates
Elevators
Schindler
Internal wooden flooring
Gazzotti
External wooden paving
F2 parquet
Marble
Casone - Bosisio
Ceramic tiles – bathroom and plumbing fixtures
Pozzi Ginori - Kaldewei - Teuco
Technical systems
Panzeri S.p.A. mechanical systems
Diesse electrical systems
Total surface area
5,180 square metres
Photography
Marco Introini

Porta Nuova Varesine Business District
Architectural project design
Kohn Pederson Fox Associates
Construction company
Stahlbau Pichler
Client
Hines Italia SGR S.p.a. and Galotti
www.kpf.com
Diamond Tower
Building
30 storeys above ground (top 3 storeys, technical services) and 4 underground storeys
Available office space
About 32,500 square metres
Retail space
271 square metres
LEED certification
Gold Certificate
Buildings 1 and 2:
Building
9 storeys above ground and 4 underground storeys

Available office space
About 12,500 square metres per building
Retail space
852 square metres per building
LEED certification
Gold Certificate

Porta Nuova Varesine
Time span
2006–2014
Status
Completed
Team leader
LAND Milano S.r.l.
Designer
Andreas Kipar
Team LAND Group
Valerio Bozzoli Parasacchi, Giuliano Garello, Valeria Pagliaro, Anna Brambilla, Elisa Frappi, Ivan Maestri
Client
Hines Italia SGR S.p.a., Porta Nuova Varesine
www.landsrl.com
Le Ville di Porta Nuova (residential complex)
Studio M2P Associati
Photography
Marco Garofalo

Gioiaotto (Office building) Via Melchiorre Gioia
Project
Park Associati (Filippo Pagliani, Michele Rossi)
with General Planning srl
Design Team Park Associati
Alessandro Rossi (project leader), Alexia Caccavella, Marinella Ferrari, Marco Panzeri, Davide Pojaga, Elisa Taddei, Paolo Uboldi, Fabio Calciati (rendering)
Work site supervision, structural, mechanical and electrical engineering.
General Planning, Milano
Team
Loris Colombo, Giuseppe Monti, Walter Cola, Luca Dagrada, Sergio Fiorati, Paolo Gardella, Danilo Gibertini, Annagiulia Gregori, Mara Olgiati, Franco Pesci, Francesco Prennushi, Paolo Rossanigo, Roberto Villa
Work site supervision
Studio Ing. Ceruti
Artistic direction
Park Associati, Arch. Alessandro Rossi
Project management
Coima Srl, Milano
Landscaping project
Land Srl
Consultants:
LEED certification
Greenwich Srl
Fire prevention consulting
GAE Engineering, Torino
Ing. Amaro
Safety consulting
General Planning, Milano
Ing. Vittorio Viganò
Contractors:
Main contractor
C.E.S.I. Società Cooperativa
Photography
Andrea Martiradonna
Park Associati
Alessandro Sartori
Marco Garofalo (p. 71)

Porta Nuova Isola
Boeri Studio, Inside Outside, William McDonough + Partners, Lucien Lagrange Architects, Baukuh Architetti
Bosco Verticale (Apartment building)
Architectural project design
Boeri Studio (Stefano Boeri, Gianandrea Barreca, Giovanni La Varra)
Landscaping project
Emanuela Borio and Laura Gatti
Developer
Hines Italia
Works supervision
Francesco de Felice, Davor Popovic
Design development
Gianni Bertoldi (coordinator), Alessandro Agosti, Andrea Casetto, Matteo Colognese, Angela Parrozzani, Stefano Onnis
Schematic design and Integrated intervention program
Frederic de Smet (coordinator), Daniele Barillari, Marco Brega, Julien Boitard, Matilde Cassani, Andrea Casetto, Francesca Cesa Bianchi, Inge Lengwenus, Corrado Longa, Eleanna Kotsikou, Matteo Marzi, Emanuela Messina, Andrea Sellanes
Project stages
2006-2009
Construction stages
2010-2014
Structures
Arup Italia s.r.l.
Technical systems
Deerns Italia S.p.A.
Detailed project
Tekne s.p.a.
Project Open Space
Land s.r.l.
Infrastructures
Alpina S.p.A.
Contract administration
MI.PR.AV. s.r.l.
Incubatore per l'arte (cultural centre)
Project Team
Boeri Studio (Stefano Boeri, Gianandrea Barreca, Giovanni La Varra)
Chiara Quinzii (project leader), Marco Brega (Project coordinator)
Collaborating contractors
Alessandro Agosti, Daniele Barillari, Frederic De Smet, Kristina Drapic, Marco Giorgio, Inge Lengwenus
Project Time span
2006-2009
Construction time span
2010-2013
Client
Hines Italia SGR S.p.A
Contractor
Coim srl
Technical Consultants
Tekne srl
Photography
Iwan Baan

Porta Nuova Isola
Time span
2012
Status
Completed
Client
Hines Italia SGR S.p.a.
Team leader
LAND Milano S.r.l.
Designer
Andreas Kipar
Team LAND Group
Valerio Bozzoli Parasacchi, Giuliano Garello, Ivan Maestri
La Biblioteca degli Alberi (Park)
Project
Inside Outside
Business District Isola
Project
William McDonough + Partners
Residenze dei Giardini (Residential complex)
Project
Lucien Lagrange Architects
Casa Della Memoria (Museum)
Project
Baukuh Architetti
Con dotdotdot, Stefano Graziani, Amedeo Martegani, Giovanna Silva
Centro civico (Civic centre)
Designers
KM 429 architettura (Simona Avigni – Alessio Bernardelli Architetti), Francesco Pergetti Architect, Serena Manfredi Architects
www.km429architettura.com
Client
Comune di Milano
Time span
2014 competition in 2 stages
Surface area
900 square metres

V33
Residential building
Via Volturno 33
Project design and Artistic direction
Vudafieri Saverino Partners (Tiziano Vudafieri and Claudio Saverino)
www.vudafierisaverino.it
Team
Massimo Nebuloni, Roberta La Vena, Luca Mucciante, Raffaella Barbera, Licia Belfi, Roberta Pezzulla
Structural project design
Studio Integral
Technical systems
Studio PGS ingegneria
Permits and authorisations, Site manager
Studio A&U
Project management
Studio Starching
Construction company
ZH Milano
Client
Hobag
Photography
Filippo Romano

Istituto Gonzaga (High Scool) Via Vitruvio/Via Settembrini
Project
One Works
Client
Istituto Gonzaga. Provincia di Torino della Congregazione dei Fratelli delle Scuole Cristiane. Roberto Cottini - Project representative
Client
Vitruvio Immobiliare srl
Architectural project design
One Works - Leonardo Cavalli, Michele Pugliese, Davide De Giobbi, Antonio Romanò, Luigi Pezzotta
Structural project design
One Works - Gianluigi Santinello, Riccardo Pauletto, Nicola Padoan
Geotechnical consultants
Lombardi – Reico
Site manager
One Works - Gianluigi Santinello, Davide De Giobbi, Riccardo Pauletto, Luigi Pezzotta, Vito Vernavà

Construction company
Associazione Temporanea d'Imprese, Morganti Construction company SpA, Impresa Rosso SpA, Vitruvio Immobiliare srl
Technical systems
QB Service - Luca Mioliggi, Andrea Nicola
Technical lighting project
Ferrara Palladino e Associati - Cinzia Ferrara
Acoustics
L.C.E. srl - Claudio Costa
Fire prevention
Studio Tecnico Zaccarelli srl
Photography
Studio ORCH - Fulvio Orsenigo

City Pavilion
Piazza Duca d'Aosta
Project
Tiziano Vudafieri – Claudio Saverino
Vudafieri Saverino Partners Milano-Shanghai
Client
Shanghai-Milano Fashion & Design Hub
Project Team
Elisa Zhu, Luca Mucciante
Project Manager
Marcello Rossi
Construction project and general operational development
Plotini Allestimenti
Furnishing supplier
MDF Italia
Lighting supplier
Guzzini
Door supplier
Lualdi
Bar counter supplier
Grandimpianti Ali, Fratelli Bianchi
Window dressing
Oltrefrontiera Progetti
Graphic communications
Hangar Design Group
Sponsors: Expo Milano 2015, City of Milan, City of Shanghai
Photography
Santi Caleca

Outskirts of Milan

MUDEC – Museo delle Culture (Museum)
Via Tortona
MUDEC – Comune di Milano
Director of the Modern and Contemporary art centre
Marina Pugliese
Head of administration
Eugenio Petz
Collection conservators
Museo delle Culture - Area ex Ansaldo
Carolina Orsini, Iolanda Ratti, Omar Cucciniello
Conservation department, Loan department
Luciana Gerolami, Cristina Filippi
Administration department
Elisa Errico, Eugenio Arcieri
Technical department
Giuseppe Braga
Secretariat
Laura Tommencioni, Susi Silvestre
Librarian
Giulia Gaudiano
Modern and Contemporart Art Centre –Communications Manager
Clementina Rizzi
Comune di Milano - Press Office
Elena Conenna
MUDEC – 24 ORE Cultura (Cultural centre)
President
Donatella Treu
CEO
Natalina Costa
Mudec Director
Simona Serini
Exhibition department director
Francesca Biagioli
Exhibition department Production and organisation
Francesca Calabretta, Alberta Crestani, Silvia Iannelli
Registrar
Sandra Serafini
Communications
Sara Lombardini
Bookshop
Roberta Proserpio, Greta Bortolotti, Marta Miglierina
Ticket office and other services
With the contribution of Elena Stella
Fundraising department director, events and special initiatives
Chiara Giudice
Fundraising, events and special initiatives
Francesca Belli
With the contribution of Valeria Canelli, Marica Gagliardi, Marilù Manta, Giulia Mordivoglia, Massimo Navoni, Letizia Rossi, Ilaria Villani
Development office
Paola Cappitelli
With the contribution of Lucia Benaglio
Social Media and Press Office
With the contribution of Michela Beretta, Stefania Coltro, Barbara Notaro Dietrich
Operations Manager
Alessandro Volpi
Operations department
Elena Colombini, Elisabetta Colombo, Giorgia Montagna
With the contribution of Andrea Baraldi, Valentina Vasamì
Publishing manager
Balthazar Pagani
Editor
Chiara Savino
Publishing department
Nicoletta Grassi, Chiara Bellifemine
International rights and distribution
Simona Scuri
Managing editor
Giuseppe Scandiani
Editorial department
Stefania Vadrucci
Technical and graphics department manager
Maurizio Bartomioli
Iconographic department manager
Gian Marco Sivieri
IconoGraphics research
Alessandra Murolo
Photography
© Photo OskarDaRiz

CityLife
Piazzale Giulio Cesare (residential, commercial and business district)
Zaha Hadid LTD, Arata Isozaki & Associates, Studio Daniel Libeskind
Residenze Libeskind
Designers
Join Venture Studio Daniel Libeskind New York with Libeskind Architettura s.r.l., Milano
Structural project design
Agenzia Milano Strutture s.r.l.
Mechanical engineering
Manens Intertecnica and Hilson Moran Italia S.p.A
Landscaping project
Marsiglilab, Margherita Brianza, Enzo Paoli
Coordination
Alpina S.p.A
Main contractor
City Contractor s.c.a.r.l.
Constructors
Landscape
Euroambiente
Wooden doors and windows
Dallera S.p.A.
Windows
Focchi S.p.A.
Facade
Tempini- Frattini
Suppliers
Porcelain stoneware cladding
Casalgrande Padana
External paving
Graniti Fiandre
Window and door frames
Schuco International and Metra
Lighting
Zumtobel
Lobby furnishing
Cassina Contract
Elevators
Schindler
Doors and handles
Tre-p Tre-più, Olivari
WPC decking
Woodn and Greenwood
Sustainability
CENED A+
Photography
Alberto Fanelli
Residenze Hadid
CityLife (Residential complex)
Project
Zaha Hadid Architects
Project direction
Gianluca Racana
Project Manager
Maurizio Meossi
Project team
Vincenzo Barilari, Cristina Capanna, Giacomo Sanna, Paola Bettinsoli, Gianluca Bilotta, Fabio Ceci, Veronica Erspamer, Arianna Francioni, Stefano Iacopini, Mario Mattia, Serena Pietrantonj, Florindo Ricciuti, Giulia Scaglietta, Giovanna Sylos Labini, Anja Simons, Marta Suarez, Tamara Tancorre, Giuseppe Vultaggio, Massimiliano Piccinini, Samuele Sordi, Alessandra Belia
Worksite supervision
Cristina Capanna, Veronica Erspamer, Stefano Iacopini, Giulia Scaglietta, Florindo Ricciuti
Competition team
Simon Kim, Yael Brosilovski, Adriano De Gioannis, Graham Modlen, Karim Muallem, Daniel Li, Yang Jingwen, Tiago Correia, Ana Cajiao, Daniel Baerlecken, Judith Reitz
Photography
Alberto Fanelli, © Photo Up

Torre Allianz
CityLife
Architectural project design
Arata Isozaki with Andrea Maffei
Architectural project construction
Colombo Costruzioni S.p.A
Mpartners S.r.l.
Structural project construction
Colombo Costruzioni S.p.A.
Studio Ecsd (prof. Franco Mola)
Studio Iorio (prof. Francesco Iorio)
Studio Capé
Technical systems construction
Colombo Costruzioni S.p.A.
Studio Ariatta
Site manager
IN.PRO.SRL and Ingegneria Spm (ing. Claudio Guido)
Structural inspections
CE.A.S. Srl (ing. Bruno Finzi)
Civil works inspections
Studio Ingegneria Rigone (prof. Paolo Rigone)
Technical systems inspections
Manens Tifs S.p.A (ing. Giorgio Marchioretti)
Main contractor
Colombo Costruzioni S.p.A.
Time span
32 months
Photography
Alberto Fanelli

Piazza Tre Torri
CityLife
Architect
One Works
Client
Citylife
Technical lighting project
Ferrara Palladino e Associati
Structural work
Holzner & Bertagnolli Engineering srl
Green areas
Studio Laura Gatti
Systems installation
Ariatta Ingegneria dei Sistemi S.r.l.
Rendering
Struttura Leggera, Lin Render

Portello area redevelopment
Viale Scarampo
Studio Valle Architetti Associati, Cino Zucchi Architetti, Zucchi & Partners, Canali Associati, Charles Jencks, Andreas Kipar – LAND, Topotek 1, Arup
IPER Montebello Spa
Real Estate developer
Ennio Brion
Urban Masterplan, Architectural project: retail and offices
Studio Valle Architetti Associati
Residential architecture
Cino Zucchi Architetti, Zucchi & Partners; Canali Associati
Urban park landscaping
Charles Jencks con Andreas Kipar - LAND
Arial photography
FOTO UP (Monza)
Photography
Marco Introini, Cino Zucchi

IULM Language and Communication University, Knowledge Transfer Center, KTC
Via Carlo Bo
Project
5+1AA Alfonso Femia Gianluca Peluffo
Client
IULM – Libera Università di Lingue e Comunicazione
Architects
Alfonso Femia, Gianluca Peluffo with Alessandro Schiesaro
Security surveillance
Cesare Stevan
Angelo Bugatti
Structural engineering
IQuadro ingegneria
Technical systems engineering
Deerns Italia spa
Fire prevention
Studio Tecnico Zaccarelli
Project Manager
Luca Pozzi
Project team
Gabriele Pulselli, Raffaella F. Pirrello, Daniele Marchetti, Domenica Laface, Alessandro Bellus, Lorenza Barabino, Luca Pozzi
Program
Extension of IULM (Libera Università di Lingue e Comunicazione): tower: spaces for laboratories and research; north building: cafeteria and kitchens for the whole IULM campus; South building: lecture halls, laboratories and offices, auditorium (capacity 600)
Total surface
23,261 square metres
Gross surface area
9,950 square metres
Time span
2003-2014
Model
Danilo Trogu
Photography
© Ernesta Caviola
Awards
Special mention at the "AIT International Awards 2014" in Frankfurt (Germany)

Prada Foundation Headquarters
Largo Isarco
OMA/Rem Koolhaas
Team OMA
Partners
Rem Koolhaas, Chris van Duijn
Project leader
Federico Pompignoli
Project area
Total constructed surface
18,900 square metres
Area open to the public
12,300 square metres
Area not accessible to the public
6,600 square metres
Total exhibition surface
11,146 square metres
Exhibition space in pre-existant buildingsi
7,100 square metres
Exhibition space in new buildings
4,046 square metres
Rendering
Courtesy of OMA and Fondazione Prada
Photography
Bas Princen 2015, courtesy of Fondazione Prada

Carlo Erba Residential complex
Piazza Carlo Erba
Project
2010-2011; construction: 2012 – ongoing construction
Architectural project design
Eisenman Architects (Peter Eisenman, Richard Rosson), New York
Degli Esposti Architetti (Lorenzo Degli Esposti, Paolo Lazza, Stefano Antonelli), Milano
AZstudio (Guido Zuliani), Udine
Structural project design
Studio d'Ingegneria Associato Ardolino, Bolzano
Technical systems design
Sistema Group Engineergin s.r.l., Montichiari
Construction company
C.L.E. – Cooperativa Lavoratori Edili Società Cooperativa, Bolzano
Security and surveillance
Sherpa Engineering s.r.l., Mantova
Proprietor
Pinerba s.r.l.

Residential buildings
Via Tiraboschi
Architectural project design and Site manager
Beretta Associati Srl
Client
Massena Real Estate Srl
Year
2013
Contract manager
Arch. Federico Aldini
Construction company
Impresa Minotti Srl
Coordination
Arch. Paolo Montorfano
Structural project
Ing. Giulio Farina
Technical systems
BRE Engineering Srl - Ing. Gianpiero Bozino
Gross surface area
3,070 square metres
Photography
Andrea Martiradonna

Montegani Residential complex
Via Montegani
Project
Piuarch, Francesco Fresa, Germán Fuenmayor, Gino Garbellini, Monica Tricario
Constructed surface area
15,300 square metres
Client
Minneapolis S.r.l
Structural project design
FV Progetti S.n.c.
Technical systems design
Flu.project Studio Associato
Technical lighting project
Rossi Bianchi Lighting Design

La Forgiatura (Business school campus)
Via Varesina 158
Project
Arch. Giuseppe Tortato
Client
La Forgiatura S.r.l., Milano
Developer
Realstep property management
Process manager
Marco Bettalli
Project team
Marco Bettalli, Giorgia Celli, Barbara Storchi, Antonio Urru
Construction project
A&I progetti, Stefano Niccoli
Structural project design
Biesse Consulting, Bruno Salesi

Technical systems
Tekser S.r.l., Stefano De Marchi
Landscaping project
AG&P
Site manager
Carlo Bossi, Alberto Rizzo
Main contractor
G.D.M. costruzioni S.p.a.
Photography
Andrea Puggiotto, Stefano Topuntoli

Greater Milan

Cascina Merlata – Expo Village
Via Capo Rizzuto
Antonio Citterio Patricia Viel and Partners, Caputo Partnership, MCA Mario Cucinella Architects, Teknoarch, CZA Cino Zucchi Architetti, C+S Associati, Pura, B22
Masterplan "Cascina Merlata": Integrated intervention program
Urban planning
Antonio Citterio Patricia Viel and Partners
Caputo Partnership
Infrastructures and roading.
Proiter srl
Traffic flow analysis
TRM Engineering srl
Landscaping - Park, piazzas, green areas
Arch. Franco Giorgietta
Arch. Giovanna Longhi
Cascina Merlata Restoration
Caputo Partnership
School complex (competition by invitation)
Onsite studio
Social Housing Lotto R9/Expo Village
Architectural project design
Buildings 1, 2, 7 Mca:
M. Cucinella, D. Hirsch, M. Dell'Agli, L. Stramigioli, G. Maggio
Buildings. 9 10 Teknoarch:
D. Piludu, B. Licheri, C. Sanna, F. Di Lalla, L. Di Benedetto
Building. 5 Pura: M. Parini, E. Roy Nash
Building 11 B22: S. Tropea, M. M. Mugica
Structural construction project
Intertecno
Sca Project S.r.l.
Technical systems installation
Qb service s.r.l., Ciriè (Torino)
Coprat
Ariatta Ingegneria dei Sistemi srl
Construction companies
Covexpo s.c.a.r.l. (CMB - Cile - Mangiavacchi Pedercini - Nessi & Majocchi)
Execution
2012-2015
Social Housing second stage
Building 3, 4 CZA: C. Zucchi, A. Viganò, M. Corno, I. Bergamaschi, O. d. Ciuceis, C. Molinari, L. Torri
Buildings A and B, Lot R11
C+S: C. Cappai, M. A. Segantini

Milanofiori Nord
Assago (Milan)
Project
Designed by Erick van Egeraat
www.eea-architects.com
Landscape project
Amber architectures, Massimo Bertolano
Client
Milanofiori 2000 srl (Gruppo Brioschi Sviluppo Immobiliare)
Photography
Maurizio Bianchi
Shopping malls Milanofiori Nord
Architectural project and Landscaping
5+1AA Alfonso Femia Gianluca Peluffo
www.5piu1aa.com
Designers
Alfonso Femia, Gianluca Peluffo, Simonetta Cenci
Structural engineering
IQuadro ingegneria
Technical engineering
Marco Taccini
Integrated engineering work / Site manager
Tekne srl
Artistic direction
5+1AA Alfonso Femia Gianluca Peluffo
Civil works
A.T.I. tra Unionbau S.r.l. e PFB S.p.A., Prefabricated and reinforced concrete structures: IPA Precast S.p.A., Temporary contract electrical and mechanical installations: Gianni Benvenuto S.p.A. and Atel Sesti S.p.A.
Project Manager
Gabriele Filippi
Design team
Francesca Ameglio, Cinzia Avanzi, Lorenza Barabino, Luca Bonsignorio, Stefania Bracco, Yulia Breslav, Francesca Calcagno, Domenico Conaci, Magda Di Domenico, Enrico Martino, Sara Massa, Nicola Montera, Carola Picasso, Francesca R. Pirrello, Alessandra Quarello, Francesca Recagno, Ilaria Sisto, Laura Vallino
Client
Milanofiori 2000 srl (Gruppo Brioschi Sviluppo Immobiliare)
Photography
Maurizio Bianchi
Milanofiori Nord Residential complex
Project
OBR Open Building Research S.r.l., Paolo Brescia, Tommaso Principi
www.openbuildingresearch.com
Design team
Chiara Pongiglione, François Doria, Paolo Salami, Giulia D'Ettorre, Julissa Gutarra, Leonardo Mader, Francesco Vinci, Barbara Zuccarello
Consultants during project stage
Buro Happold (energy and environmental strategies), Favero & Milan Ingegneria (Structures and cost control), StudioT.I. (systems installation), LAV S.r.l. (acoustic testing)
General Site Manager
Favero & Milan Ingegneria (Alessandro Bonaventura, Alessandro Orlandi)
Artistic direction
OBR Open Building Research S.r.l. (Paolo Brescia, Chiara Pongiglione, François Doria)
Construction safety coordination
Romeo S.r.l. (Damiano Romeo, Stefano Misiano)
Contracting company
A.T.I. Marcora Costruzioni S.p.a - Cile S.p.a.
Client
Milanofiori 2000 srl (Gruppo Brioschi Sviluppo Immobiliare)
Photography
Maurizio Bianchi
Milanofiori Nord U15 Office building
Project
CZA - Cino Zucchi Architetti
www.zucchiarchitetti.com
Architectural project and Artistic direction
Cino Zucchi Architetti - Cino Zucchi, Sarah Zezza, Michele Corno, Laura Gusso, Valentina Zanoni with Filippo Carcano, Diego Martinelli, Stefano Goffi, Maria Silvia Di Vita and Filippo Facchinetto - rendering
Main contractor
ZH General Construction Company AG/SPA
Werner Zimmerhofer, Gustav Clara; Christian Obermair
Final project design, construction work and general site manager.
General Planning S.r.l.
Giovanni Bonini, Loris Colombo, Paolo Varenna, Laura Barat, Marta Franzelli Matteo Molteni, Luca Dagrada, Paolo Rossanigo, Alberto Villa, Walter Cola
Client
Milanofiori 2000 srl (Gruppo Brioschi Sviluppo Immobiliare)
Photography
Maurizio Bianchi
Milanofiori Nord Subsidized housing
Project
ABDAarchitetti botticini – de appolonia & associati
www.abdarchitetti.com
Client
Bright srl
Photography
Maurizio Bianchi
Milanofiori Nord U27 Office buildings
Architectural project and Artistic direction
Park Associati (Filippo Pagliani, Michele Rossi)
www.parkassociati.com
General project,civil and structural construction and technical system installation
General Planning, Milano
Site manager and safety aspects
General Planning, Milano
Main contractor
Milanofiori 2000 srl
Facades
Focchi Spa, Poggio Berni (Rn)
LEED Certification
General Planning, Milano; Greenwich Srl,Medolago (BG)
Park Associati Design team
Filippo Pagliani, Michele Rossi, Marco Siciliano, project leader; Marinella Ferrari, Stefano Lanotte, Marco Panzeri, Davide Pojaga, Alessandro Rossi, Elisa Taddei, Paolo Uboldi, Fabio Calciati, rendering
General Planning project team
Giovanni Bonini (RL, DL), Paolo Varenna, project leader; Loris Colombo, Laura Barat, Matteo Molteni, Luca

Dagrada, Paolo Rossanigo, Alberto Villa, Claudio Bertolini, Luigi Zinco, Walter Cola, Andrea Cristaldi, Vittorio Viganò (CS), Claudio Bertagnolli, Manuel Schieder, Mario Pinoli, Giuseppe Zaffino
Client
Milanofiori 2000 srl (Gruppo Brioschi Sviluppo Immobiliare)
Photography
Andrea Martiradonna

Daisaku Ikeda New Cultural Centre for Peace Via Marchesi, Corsico (Milan)
Peia Associati Srl - arch. Giampiero Peia, arch. Marta Nasazzi
Intervention area
Historic building gross total surface area;
new construction gross total surface area.
36,000 square metres 4,200 square metres 1,800 square metres
6,000 square metres on 10,000 square metre achievable area.
Proprietor
Soka Gakkai Italian Buddhist Institute
Construction company
G.D.M. Costruzioni S.p.a. - Vittadello Intercantieri S.p.a.
Project design
Peia associati S.r.l.
Architectural designer and artistic director
Arch. Giampiero Peia
Structural designer
Ai Engineering s.r.l. - ing. Gabriele Chiellino
Technical systems designer
Ai Engineering s.r.l. - ing. Stefano Cremo, Enrico Fabris
Project manager
Ai Engineering s.r.l. - ing. Adriano Venturini
General survey
Arch. Colombo Zefinetti
Material survey
Arch. Peverelli
Project design team for preliminary restoration stage
Arch. Giampiero Peia, arch. Giancarlo Leone and Enrico Colosimo
Complete construction time span
Start of construction: July 2011 – End of construction: July 2014
Suppliers:
Lighting
Martini Illuminazione
Steel and bronze window frames
Secco sistemi Spa
bathroom fixtures
Cisal
Porcelain stoneware floors and cladding
Casal Grande Padana – FGM
Graniti Fiandre
Rainscreen facade
Palagio Engineering
Glass walls
AGC Europe
Special paint finishes
Oikos
Furnishing
Paolo Castelli - Moroso - Vitra
Sliding panels
Anaunia
Traditional plaster finish
Gasparoli
External paving and parking areas
Magnetti
Mechanical and plumbing installations
Gianni Benvenuto
Electrical installation
DS Electra
Photography
Beppe Raso, Alberto Strada (+ Drone), Giampiero Peia

New Holding Humanitas office building Rozzano (Milan)
Project
FTA | Filippo Taidelli Architetto
Client
ICH - Istituto Clinico Humanitas
Structural project design
Terzini Ingegneria
Mechanical systems
Tecva S.r.l.
Electrical systems
Tecnoimpianti 2000
Technical lighting project
Rossi Bianchi Lighting Design
Landscaping
Area 68 S.a.s.
Main contractor
Respedil S.r.l.
Status
Completed
Photography
Andrea Martiradonna
Ich Campus
Rozzano (Milano)
Project
FTA| Filippo Taidelli Architetto
Program
New University Campus
Client
ICH - Istituto Clinico Humanitas
Surface area
22,000 square metres
Status
Preliminary project

Biblioteca civica "Vittorio Sereni" (Public library) Via Agnese Pasta 43, Melzo (Milan)
Construction program, preliminary architectural project, internal decor and furnishing, artistic direction
Alterstudio Partners, Milano - www.alterstudiopartners.com
Gross surface area
2,100 square metres
Public areas and green spaces
900 square metres
Client
Comune di Melzo
Project
2008-2010
Construction
2011-2014
Capacity
About 130 (40 at work desks)
Construction, structural project and technical systems, Site manager, Site safety coordination
SERV.E.T. Srl, Crema - www.servetsrl.it
Graphics and visual communications project
Pietro Corraini - www.pietrocorraini.com
Construction company
Arm Engineering SpA, Vigonza (PD)
www.arm-engineering.it
Furnishing supplies
Tecnocoop srl - www.tecnocoopsrl.it
RFID and self-service systems
Bibliotheca RFID Library Systems
Photography
Marco Bottani

MedaTeca - New Meda public library Via Gagarin 13, Meda (Monza e Brianza)
Project
Alterstudio Partners
Client
Comune di Meda
Project
2008–2009
Construction
2010–2011
Inauguration
April 2012
Awards and citations
Gold Medal finalist for Italian Architecture 2012
Construction program, Architectural project and furnishing, Site manager
Alterstudio Partners (arch. Marco Muscogiuri, designer and project manager), with ing. Marco Bonomi (construction site manager assistance) and ing. Oscar Pagani (construction stage safety coordination), arch. Antonio Galeano (Facade construction project)
Structural Project and Site manager
Ing. Enrico Busnelli
Technical systems Project and Site manager
Teknema Consulting srl
Library science program
Alessandro Agustoni
Graphics and visual communications
Benedetta De Bartolomeis
Decorative graphics
Mook
Art works
Francesca Zoboli
Construction company
Steda SpA
Furnishing supplies
Abaco Forniture srl
Technical sponsor
Artemide SpA, B&B Italia SpA
Photography
Marco Introini
Gross flooring surface area
1,910 square metres
Designer furnishings
Abaco Forniture, Abstracta, Arper, B&B Italia, BCI, Blå Station, Bralco Engelbrechts, Ire Mobel, Lammhults, Moroso, Offect
Lighting
Artemide, Delta Light, Fosnova, Martinelli
Window frames and glass walls
Schüco: low-emission magentronic windows composed of two glass panels with triple glazing and argon gas filled cavity.
Vetro Saint Gobain. Custom-designed matrix for customised extruded aluminium brise-soleil slatting.
Facade
System designed, customised and engineered specifically for this building. Façade system stratigraphics, bearing structure in extruded aluminium profiles (Metra extruded aluminium profiles);

press-folded, powder coated, pre-painted aluminium tile cladding; Compact rock wool insulated back panels, insulation.

Music School
Cassano d'Adda (Milan)
Architectural project
Dap Studio, Elena Sacco, Paolo Danelli
Client
Comune di Cassano D'Adda
Time span
Project 2013
Lavori 2014/2015
Coordination
Paolo Danelli
Structural Project design
Giovanbattista Scolari
Technical systems project
Ebner Engineering
Intervention category
Construction of new building and external area project design
Construction program
Auditorium, Civic music school, offices, bar, bookshop, additional spaces.
Surface area
Building: 3,000 square metres
External space: 5,000 square metres

House in the plains
Gropello Cairoli (Pavia)
Architectural project
deamicisarchitetti
Client
Private owner
Time span
2009-2012
Coordination
deamicisarchitetti
Project team
deamicisarchitetti
Structural project
Studio Stefano Galbiati
Technical systems
Studio Energy Save
Intervention category
Single family home with garden in suburban housing development
Surface area
460 square metres
Photography
L. Bartoli, G. Leo

Expo 2015

Arid zone Cluster
Expo Milano 2015
Project coordination:
Alessandro Biamonti, Michele Zini. *Collaborating universities* Politecnico di Milano, Escuela Tecnica Superior de Arquitectura de Madrid, Birzeit University in Palestine
Designers
A. Biamonti, M. Zini con B. Camocini
Collaborating contractors
S. Callioni, A. Cattabriga, S. Longaretti, S. Michelini, C. Zoboli
Scientific director
L. Collina
Content development
Politecnico di Milano
Client
Expo 2015 S.p.A.
Photography
Marco Introini

Biomediterraneum Cluster
Expo Milano 2015
Project coordination
Stefano Guidarini, Camillo Magni, Cherubino Gambardella, Lorenzo Capobianco
Collaborating universities:
Politecnico di Milano, Seconda Università degli Studi di Napoli, American University in Cairo (Egypt)
Designers
C. Gambardella, S. Guidarini, C. Magni con L. Capobianco, S. Ottieri
Collaborating contractors
V. Di Gioia, G. Ferriero, M. Gelvi, C. Tavoletta, R. Spreafico, L. Varvello, F.M.G. Vozza
Scientific director
C. Gambardella
Content development
Seconda Università degli Studi di Napoli
Client
Expo 2015 S.p.A.

Cocoa and Chocolate Cluster
Expo Milano 2015
Project coordination: Fabrizio Leoni, Mauricio Cardenas, Cesare Ventura.
Collaborating universities:
Politecnico di Milano, Itesem - Tecnologico de Monterrey (Mexico), SUPSI Lugano (Switzerland)
Designers
F. Leoni, M. Cardenas with C. Ventura
Collaborating contractors
L. De Stasio, M. Tengattini
Scientific director
P.S. Cocconcelli
Content development
Università Cattolica del Sacro Cuore
Client
Expo 2015 S.p.A.
Photography
Marco Introini

Coffee Cluster
Expo Milano 2015
Project coordination:
Armando Colombo, Stefan Vieths.
Collaborating universities:
Politecnico di Milano, Fau-Universidade de Sao Paulo (Brazil)
Designers
A. Colombo, S. Vieths
Collaborating contractors
F. Rapisarda, A. Hepner, M.N. Mainini, S. Pomodoro
Scientific director
C. Mauri
Content development
Università Bocconi, Illy
Client
Expo 2015 S.p.A.
Photography
Marco Introini, Filippo Romano

Cereals and Tubers Cluster
Expo Milano 2015
Project coordination:
Alessandro Rocca, Franco Tagliabue.
Collaborating universities:
Politecnico di Milano, Parsons School of Design, New York (USA), MARKHI-Moscow Institute of Architecture (Russia)
Project
A. Rocca, F. Tagliabue
Collaborating contractors
M. Cipriani, M. Feller, M. Geroldi, I. Origgi
Collaborating universities
Scientific director
F. Bonomi, C. Gandolfi, G.V. Zuccotti
Content development
Università degli Studi di Milano
Client
Expo 2015 S.p.A.

Fruits and Legumes Cluster
Expo Milano 2015
Project coordination:
Massimo Ferrari, Matteo Vercelloni.
Collaborating universities:
Politecnico di Milano, Cape Peninsula University of Technology in Capetown (South Africa), The Bezalel Academy of Art and Design (Israel)
Designers
M. Ferrari, M. Vercelloni
Collaborating contractors
S. De Feudis, S. Sala, C. Tinazzi
Scientific director
R. Mordacci
Content development
Università Vita e Salute San Raffaele
Client
Expo 2015 S.p.A.
Photography
Marco Introini

Spices Cluster
Expo Milano 2015
Project coordination: Michele Brunello, Pierluigi Salvadeo, Benno Albrecht.
Collaborating universities:
Politecnico di Milano, Università Iuav di Venezia, Nid-National Institute of Design (India)
Designers
M. Brunello, P. Salvadeo
Collaborating contractors
S. Bertolotti, G. Ciocoletto, G. Dogliotti, C. Longa, M. Muraro, M. Savino, R. Spreafico, L. Varvello
Scientific director
B. Albrecht
Content development
Università IUAV di Venezia
Client
Expo 2015 S.p.A.
Photography
Marco Introini, Filippo Romano

Islands, Sea and Food Cluster
Expo Milano 2015
Project coordination: Marco Imperadori, Giuliana Iannaccone. *Università:*
Politecnico di Milano, Aalto University of Helsinki (Finland), University of Tokyo (Japan)
Designers
G. Ianaccone, M. Imperadori
Collaborating contractors
V. Gallotti, S.G. Liotta, P. Trivini, A. Vanossi
Scientific director
V. Russo
Content development
Università di Lingue e Comunicazione - IULM Milano
Client
Expo 2015 S.p.A.
Photography
Marco Introini, Tom Corsan

Rice Cluster
Expo Milano 2015
Project coordination: Agnese

Rebaglio, Davide Crippa, Barbara Di Prete.
Collaborating universities:
Politecnico di Milano, Tongij University Shanghai (China), National University of Civil Engineering, Hanoi (Vietnam)
Designers
A. Rebaglio, D. Crippa, B. Di Prete con L. Loglio, F. Tosi
Collaborating contractors:
P. Saluzzi
Scientific director
M. Lavitrano
Content development
Università degli Studi Milano Bicocca
Client
Expo 2015 S.p.A.
Photography
Marco Introini

The Pavilions

Pavilion 0 Milano
Expo Milano 2015
Client
Expo 2015 S.p.A.
Coordination
M. Gatto, G. Chinellato
Technical direction
P. Sibille, F. De Ciechi, M. Gianni
Curator
D. Rampello, M. Amato, S. Karadjov, E. Bignami, G. Carandini, T. Di Bernardo
Scientific consultants
S. Papi, A. Caracausi, M. Agnoletti, G. Barbera, I. Bargna
Project design coordination
Fiera Milano SpA, M. Salvi
Architectural project design
Michele De Lucchi
Collaborating contractors
Architectural project: A. Micheli (Project Manager), S. Figini, A. Drews, A. De Leonardis, M. Biffi
Structural design and technical systems
Milan Ingegneria S.r.l.
Final project design and construction
ITECO Italian Engineering Company
Contractor
P&I Project Integrator, C.M.S. S.r.l.
Site manager
Italferr S.p.A.
Project Staging Coordination
Fiera Milano SpA, M. Salvi, C. Pravettoni, S. Monaco
Project staging
G. Basili, S. Cumella
Light designer
A. Solbiati
Sound designer
M. Saroglia
Graphic designer staging
Studio Cerri & Associati, P. Cerri, A. Colombo
Structural Project and systems installation
Milan Ingegneria S.r.l.
Winning contractor: staging supply and systems installation
RTI Set Up Live S.r.l., Tecnelit SpA
Photography
Tom Vack

Italian Pavilion
Expo Milano 2015
Client
Expo 2015 S.p.A.
Architectural project design
Nemesi & Partners Srl, Arch. Michele Molè and Arch. Susanna Tradati
Intervention area
13,500 square metres
Palazzo Italia 13,275 square metres, 6 storeys above ground
Cardo 13,776 square metres, 3 storeys above ground
Energy efficiency class
Class A
Project design partners
Proger SpA, Engineering and Cost Management
Bms Progetti Srl, Structural and installation work
Prof. Ing. Livio de Santoli, energy sustainability
Main contractor Italian pavilion
Italiana Costruzioni S.p.A.
Palazzo Italia Construction company
Mantovani Group, excavations and foundations
Italiana Costruzioni S.p.A., building construction
Italcementi SpA e Styl-Comp Group, external shell
Stahlbau Pichler Srl, Shade sail canopy
Photography
Luigi Filetici

France Pavilion
Expo Milano 2015
Project
XTU | Anouk Legendre + Nicolas Desmazières | Project leader: Mathias Lukacs
Contract company
C.M.C di Ravenna _ Simonin
Client
FranceAgriMer
Pavilion surface area
3,500 square metres
Project stage collaborating contractors
Atelien Architecture
Studio Adeline Rispal
Innovision
Licht Kunst Licht
Grontmij
Oasiis
Base
Viasonora
BECP
Rendering and images
XTU | Anouk Legendre + Nicolas Desmazières | www.x-tu.com

United Kingdom Pavilion
Expo Milano 2015
Artist and creative lead
Wolfgang
Pavilion manufacture and production
Stage One
Structural engineers
Simmonds Studio Architecture
Landscape architecture and environmental engineering
BDP
Physicist and bee expert
Dr Martin Bencsik – Nottingham Trent University
Local designers (Architectural designers in Italy)
Atelier2 – Gallotti e Imperadori associati with Ing. Gian Pietro Imperadori (structural work) Digierre3 (installations) and coordination for permits and authorisations
Structural project site manager
Atelier2 – Gallotti e Imperadori associati with Ing. Gian Pietro Imperadori
Photography
UKTI Crown Copyright

Belgium Pavilion
Expo Milano 2015
Architect and exhibition designer
Patrick Genard y Asociados
info@patrickgenard.com
www.patrickgenard.com
Associates
Marc Belderbos
Sylvain Carlet, Isern Serra
Team
Bruno Conigliano
Dariela Hentschel
Christophe Siredey
Sigfrid Pascual
Diego Rey
Nathalie Meric
Silvina Cragnolino
Carolina Gomes
Ingrid Macau
Ron Calvo
SM Besix, Vanhout
www.besix.com
Engineers
Besix Design Department
www.besix.com
Cenergie www.cenergie.be
Landscape Designer
www.jnc.be JNC Internazionale
Telecomunications
Arch & Teco Ingegneria
www.arch-teco-eng.eu
Acoustics
ASM Acoustics
www.asm-acoustics.be
Photography
Filippo Romano

Germany Pavilion
Expo Milano 2015
Official Body responsible for participation
Federal Ministry for Economy and Energy
Commissioner General of the German Pavilion
Dietmar Schmitz
Vice- Commissioner General of the German Pavilion
Peter von Wesendonk
Project-manager
Markus Weichert
Construction company
Messe Frankfurt Exhibition Gmb
German Pavilion 2015 creative design, project design, and construction
ARGE Deutscher Pavillon Expo Milano 2015
Direzione ARGE
Andreas Friese, Milla & Partner
Siegfried Kaindl, Schmidhuber
Harald Dosch, Nussli
Layout, Architectural project and general works
Schmidhuber, Monaco
Content concept, exhibition and media projects
Milla & Partner, Stoccarda
Project-manager and building construction
Nussli, Roth in Nuremburg
Pavilion surface area
4,913 square metres
Exhibition surface
2,680 square metres
Rendering
© Schmidhuber, Milla & Partner

Israel Pavilion
Expo Milano 2015
Client
Israeli Ministry for Foreign Affairs, in collaboration with

the Israeli Ministries
of Finance, Tourism,
Economy and Agriculture
Architectural project and general layout
Knafo Klimor Architects
Green wall project design and execution
Green Wall Israel
Project management
AVS Avant Video Systems
Local architects and coordination
PRR Architetti
Content concept, exhibition and media projects
AVS Avant Video Systems
Structural engineering
Rokach Ashkenazi
Engineering Consultant
Energy project
Avner Vishkin engineers
Electrical project
Rafi Cohen Engineers
Interior design
Netto Design House
Artistic direction
Avi Helitovsky
Content concept design
Alon Weisbert
Local structural engineering
Engineering project
Fire prevention
Rampoldi Progetti
Security
Studio La Viola
Rendering
Knafo Klimor Architects
Photography
Filippo Romano

Czech Republic Pavilion
Expo Milano 2015
Project
Chybik+Kristof Associated Architects
Contract company
Koma Modular s.r.o.
Client
CZEXPO
Pavilion surface area
Internal surface area 1,500 square metres
Project stage collaborating contractors
Musil, Hybská architektonický atelier s.r.o.
Subtech s.r.o.
Plyko s.r.o.
Inte s.r.o.
Sportakcent s.r.o.
Progeca s.r.l.
General Site manager
Progeca s.r.l.
Artistic coordinator
Pavel Hruza
On site safety coordination
Progeca s.r.l.
Rendering
Chybik+Kristof Associated Architects, MISS3
Photography
Filippo Romano

Brazil Pavilion
Expo Milano 2015
Architectural project and interiors
Studio Arthur Casas - Arthur Casas, Gabriel Ranieri, Alexandra Kayat, Eduardo Mikowski, Alessandra Mattar, Nara Telles, Pedro Ribeiro, Raul Cano and Renata Adoni. Texts by Luiza Costa
Local architects in Italy
Stefano Pierfrancesco Pellin and Dario Pellizzari
Curators
Eduardo Biz and Rony Rodrigues
Staging, scenography and multimedia design
Atelier Marko Brajovic - Carmela Rocha and Marko Brajovic (Project Managers). André Romitelli, Martina Brusius and Milica Djordjevic (Collaborating contractors)
Architectural and structural projects, engineering
Mosae
Andrea Savoldelli, Dario Pellizzari, Klaus Scalet, Luisa Basiricò, Michele Maddalo, Stefano Pierfrancesco Pellin
Project date
2014
Construction
2015
Surface
2,384.88 square metres
Photography
Filippo Romano

USA Pavilion
Expo Milano 2015
Client
Office of Public Diplomacy within the American State Department Bureau of European and Eurasian Affairs
Project
Biber Architects
Head architect
James Biber, FAIA LEED
Local architect
Andrea Grassi
Project team
Dan Marino, Steven Grootaert, Emaan Farhound, Alberto D'Ospina, Umberto Parma, Federico Pelligrini
Kitchen Project
Jimi Yui, Yui Design
Site manager
Jessica Healy
Project Manager
Suzanne Holt
Exhibitions and educational programs
Thinc Design
Architecture and landscape design
Dlandstudio
Team: Susannah C. Drake FASLA, AIA, Architect and Landscaping, Halina Steiner, Brett Seamans, Nick Jabs

Japan Pavilion
Expo Milano 2015
Client
Jetro Japan External Trade Organization – Japanese Government
Project Concept
Atsushi Kitagawara Architects, Tokyo
Architectural, structural, and systems project,
Ishimoto Architectural & Engineering Firm, Inc. - Tokyo (N. Shuji, Y. Sakakibara, Y. Sugawara, M. Corbella, K. Yokokawa, S. Tada, S. Asahi, S. Terashima, Y. Tahara)
Iparch S.r.l. (S. Pellin)
Stain Engineering S.r.l. (A. Danesi, F. Andreatta)
Ove Arup & Partners Japan Ltd., Arup Italia S.r.l. (L. Buzzoni, T. Yoza, M. Teora)
Site manager
Ishimoto Architectural & Engineering Firm, Inc. - Tokyo (M. Corbella)
Operations management:
Iparch S.r.l.
Partners for three-dimensional wooden facade design
Ove Arup & Partners Japan Ltd. (M. Kanada, H. Yonamine, K. Goto)
Technical consultancy for three-dimensional wooden facade technological development
Atelier2 – Gallotti and Imperadori associati
Concept, staging plan and Site manager
Dentsu Inc., Tokyo
Contract company
Takenaka Europe GmbH – Italian branch
Wooden structure manufacturer
Galloppini Legnami S.r.l.
Photography
Chiara Mariska Chiodero

Mexico Pavilion
Expo Milano 2015
Architectural design
Georgina Larrea
Project
Loguer Design
Architect
Francisco López Guerra Almada
Client
Proméxico
Pavilion surface area
3,800 square metres

Chile Pavilion
Expo Milano 2015
Official representative for the Chilean Pavilion
Lorenzo Constans
Architect
Cristián Undurraga
Project Coordinator
Sebastián Mallea
Collaborating contractors
Undurraga Deves Arquitectos
Laura Signorelli
Soledad Fernández
Associate architect in Milan
Hugo Sillano
Content development
El Otro Lado Consultora
Creation and production of audiovisual material
Riolab: Francisco Arévalo
Structural engineering and special works
F&M Ingegneria LTDA: Sandro Favero
Nico Marchiori
Wooden structure
Habitat Legno
Main contractor
Valori Sarapalti
Photography
Undurraga Deves Arquitectos

China Pavilion
Expo Milano 2015
Award
First Prize
Client
Chinese Council for the Promotion of International Trade
Organiser
Expo Milano 2015
Architects
Tsinghua University & Studio Link-Arc
Head architect
Yichen Lu (Tsinghua University + Studio Link-Arc)
Associate architects
Kenneth Namkung, Qinwen Cai, Ching-Tsung Huang (Studio Link-Arc)
Project team
Mario Bastianelli, Alban Denic, Ivi Diamantopoulou,

Shuning Fan, Zachary Grzybowski, Elvira Hoxha, Dongyul Kim, Hyunjoo Lee, Aymar Mariño-Maza (Studio Link-Arc)
Local architects and engineers
F&M Ingegneria
Structural engineering
Simpson Gumpertz & Heger
Facade engineering
Elite Facade Consultants + ATLV
Technical installation project (MEP)
Beijing Qingshang Environmental Art & Architectural Design
Landscaping, staging and interior project design
Project Manager
Dan Su, Yue Zhang (Academy of Arts and Design, Tsinghua University)
Project Coordinator
Yi Du (Academy of Arts and Design, Tsinghua University)
Staging project
Yanyang Zhou, Danqing Shi (Academy of Arts and Design, Tsinghua University)
Landscaping project
Xiaosheng Cui (Academy of Arts and Design, Tsinghua University)
Interior Design
Jiansong Wang (Academy of Arts and Design, Tsinghua University)
Project installations
Danqing Shi, Feng Xian (Academy of Arts and Design, Tsinghua University)
Lighting
Yi Du (Academy of Arts and Design, Tsinghua University)
Visual identity
Xin Gu (Academy of Arts and Design, Tsinghua University)
Photography
Filippo Romano

Colombia Pavilion Expo Milano 2015
Client
Republic of Columbia
Commissioner General
Juan Pablo Cavalier Lozano
Project design
Arch. Mauricio Cardenas Laverde
Preliminary project
Arch. Manuel Villa, Arch. Antonio Yemail, I.D. Christiaan Job Nieman
Final project
Arch. Mauricio Cardenas Laverde, Ing. Monica Tengattini
Collaborating contractors
Arch. Renata Vieira, Geom. Andrea Perletti
Construction project
Arch. Mauricio Cardenas Laverde, Ing. Marcello Vecchi
Collaborating contractors
Arch. Gioacchino Pirello, Arch. Simone Riccomi
Intern
Marcos Romero
Facade project
Arch. Mauricio Cardenas Laverde, Ing. Monica Tengattini
Collaborating contractors
Arch. Renata Vieira, Arch. Daniele Tanzi
Interns
Manuela Bonilla, Candelaria Posada, Andrea Oltrabella
Exhibition project
Sistole
Execution
Project manager
Ing. Enrico Marco Rocchi
Site manager
Arch. Mauricio Cardenas Laverde, D.L. Operativa Ing. Monica Tengattini
Safety and security
Ing. Marcello Vecchi, Arch. Gioacchino Pirello
Technical supervision
Arch. Mauricio Cardenas Laverde, Geom. Andrea Perletti
Tests and inspection
Ing. Renato Vitaliani
Structural project
Ing. Angelo Benvenuti
Technological systems
Borgato Per. Ind. Alessio
Structural work
STA Ingegneri Associati
Security
TECH Srl
Electrical and mechanical systems
Sice
Main contractor
Paolo Beltrami Spa
Subcontractor
Legnolandia Srl
Project Manager
Ing. Nicola Borsella
Risk management
Geom. Simone Vitiello
Wooden structures
Ing. Loris Borean
Logistics
Giovanni Rimoldi, Daria Rimoldi
Environmental manager
Ing. Silvia Calzati
Photography
Mauricio Cardenas Laverde

Kuwait Pavilion Expo Milano 2015
Project Title
Kuwait Pavilion
Category
Exhibition pavilion
Main contractor
Nussli Italia Srl
Architect
Italo Rota
Engineering
Project CMR
Scenography
Steiner
Hydroponics
Archiverde
Locality
Expo Milano 2015, lot 39
Client
State of Kuwait, Ministry of Information
Date
Construction from June 2014 till April 2015
Organisational coordination
Nussli Italia Srl
Rendering
Studio Italo Rota

Slow Food Pavilion Expo Milano 2015
Expo 2015 Milano
Partners
Jacques Herzog, Pierre de Meuron, Andreas Fries (leading partner)
Project team
Liliana Amorim Rocha (Project Manager), Alessia Catellani, María Ángeles Lerín Ruesca (Associate), Mateo Mori, Marco Uliana
Project design and construction
Rubner Objektbau Consorzio Stabile S. with. R. L., Brunico
Photography
Filippo Romano

Intesa Sanpaolo Pavilion Expo Milano 2015
Area
1,104 square metres
Project
Architect Michele De Lucchi S.r.l. - Michele De Lucchi
Project team
Alberto Bianchi (Project Manager), Simona Agabio Matteo Di Ciommo, Francesco Faccin (studio model)
Fabio Calciati (rendering)
Client
Intesa Sanpaolo
Position
Exhibition site Expo 2015, Rho, Milan (Italy)
Project structure and technical systems
Jacobs Italia S.p.A
Structure and facade construction
L.A. Cost Srl
Construction and systems company
Esiet S.p.A.
Photography
Tom Vack

Piacenza Pavilion Expo Milano 2015
Promoter
Piacenza Expo Spa on behalf of Ats Piacenza per Expo 2015
Workshop
Politecnico di Milano – Polo Territoriale di Piacenza – Facoltà di Architettura
Prof. Guya Bertelli, coordinator
Order of Architects - P.P.C. of Piacenza
Arch. Giuseppe Baracchi, coordinator
Project team
Prof. Sandro Rolla, tutor Politecnico di Milano
Arch. Enrico De Benedetti, tutor Ordine degli Architetti P.P.C. di Piacenza
Students. Greta Andreoli, Michele Bassi, Ilaria Bianchi, Lorenzo Cocchi, Simone Varani
U35 architects: Mila Boeri, Daria Ghezzi, Marta Piana, Rosemary Ramelli, Filippo Ravera
Photography
Sandro Rolla